WICKED U

First published in Welsh in 2011 by
Gomer Press, Llandysul, Ceredigion SA44 4JL
under the title *Y Ddau Ryfel Byd Enbyd*

ISBN 978 1 84851 462 1

A CIP record for this title is available from the British Library.

This book is published with the financial support of the Welsh Books Council.

Printed and bound in Wales at Gomer Press, Llandysul, Ceredigion SA44 4JL

CONTENTS

A QUICK INTRODUCTION

Do you enjoy reading about fighting and killing, bombing and burning, gassing and ghastliness? Then THIS is the book for you. It's the story of Wicked Wales during two woeful wars in the first half of the twentieth century. BUT be warned:

BEWARE OF THIS BOOK!

Do NOT read this Wicked Welsh history in bed just before falling asleep, or you will have dreadful dreams and nasty nightmares.

Hide this book from your nosey history teachers, or they will tease and torment you with stupid questions such as:

* Because the First World War was so woeful, everyone said that this would be the last GREAT war FOREVER AND EVER, AMEN! – until the Second World War, that is!

** For many years after the Second World War people believed that Hitler was still alive, and they thought they saw men who looked like him everywhere. But don't worry. Adolf Hitler died on 30 April 1945, and he's not hiding in your school disguised as a hopeless history teacher.

But what did Wicked Wales do to help the war effort during these two terrifying World Wars?

A File of Fantastic Facts about Wales and the Wars:

We know for a fact that:

◆ 272,000 Welshmen fought for Britain during the First World War.

◆ 55,000 Welsh people were killed during the sad Second World War.

◆ Thousands worked in huge factories in Wales during the two World Wars. They made bombs and shells to kill their enemies – men, women and children right across the globe.

◆ Someone from your family – your great-great-grandpa, or great-great-grandma – probably took part in the fighting and killing. Unfortunately, because it was such a terrifying time, they don't like to remember or talk about their experiences.

What did you do during the Great War, Great-grampa?

Mmm. Not a great deal, *bach*!

But it's quite obvious that Wales did make a HUGE contribution to the fighting and killing. Good old Wales!

What happened when and where?

So many gruesome and ghastly things happened during the first half of the twentieth century that even truly talented teachers tend to get totally confused. So, since we're not quite as clever as them, we'll take one woeful war at a time.

THE WASTEFUL FIRST WORLD WAR

Another Introduction!

A TIMELINE FOR THE WASTEFUL FIRST WORLD WAR

Swallow this tedious timeline and your sad history teachers will worship you. They love boring dates and facts, and you will be their starry swot.

A TOP TIP

To digest boring dates: study them carefully for three minutes, hold your nose, close your eyes and swallow three times. Well, they do say that it's three tries for the Welsh, don't they?

1914

28 June

A stupid Serbian shoots dead Archduke Franz Ferdinand of Austria-Hungary in Sarajevo. Serbia and Austria-Hungary at war.

4 August

Germany attacks Belgium. Britain joins the war to defend little Belgium. Thousands of Welshmen rush to join the army. They believe that fighting in France will be far nicer than slaving on a farm on Anglesey, or working down a coalmine in the Rhondda!

Bye-bye, Anglesey. *Vive La France!*

The Battle of Marne

September–November

Everyone busy digging trenches across Belgium and France and getting into them to hide from the enemy — and then spending the rest of the war trying to get out of them.

1915

April

The Germans use poison gas (panic stations!) as a weapon. The Brits decide to copy this idiotic idea but the wind blows the gas back into their own trenches. Around 2,000 people choke on it (gas-p, gas-p!) and seven are killed. (Well done, Britain!)

7 May

The *Lusitania* — a luxury liner from Britain — is sunk by a German submarine and 1,198 are drowned, including 128 Americans. America furious — but this doesn't spur her into joining the fun of the fray!

1916

31 May–1 June

The Battle of Jut**land** — at sea NOT on land!

The Brilliant Battle of Jutland

Number of ships sunk:

Germany	11
Britain	15

Result: a drawn game (so they said)! Well done, everyone, except those who were drowned of course!

1 July–18 November

The great battle of the Somme. On the first day alone 20,000 British soldiers killed.

7–12 July

Capturing Mametz Wood — 4,000 Welshmen die (much more about these sobering stories under 'A Triumphant Moment for the Welsh Boys?').

15 September

Britain starts to use tanks on the Somme, but the tanks get stuck in the mud.

7 December
David Lloyd George, the LITTLE Welsh wizard,
becomes Prime Minister of GREAT Britain.

Abracadabra!

I wonder what the wily wizard has up his sleeve today?

1917
6 April
America joins the war – high time too.

16 July–November
Third Battle of 'Wipers' (Ypres at the time, Ieper
these days) — more futile fighting and killing.

31 July
The poet, Hedd Wyn, killed in the battle of
Passchendaele. (This hopeless hero's horrible history
can be found in a fantastic film. See also 'Pathetic
Portrait of a Hapless Hero'.) Britain gaining ground
very, very gradually — it would take 180 years to win
the war at this rate!

1918

11 November

The First World War ends — very cool timing — at 11 o'clock on the 11th day of the 11th month of the year!

Peace — for now!

A QUIRKY QUIZ ABOUT THE WASTEFUL FIRST WORLD WAR (1914–1918)

(Give yourself marks for each correct answer – Hip hip hooray!)

1. *Who was fighting in this war?*

(a) Everyone, in every home, village and town in the whole world!

(b) Germany, France, Britain, Russia, Australia, America, Turkey, Italy, Austria, Canada, India and . . .
(100 nations by the end); a true WORLD war.

(c) Every country except Switzerland, Sweden, Spain, the Netherlands, Denmark − and that's only in Europe. So was it really a WORLD war?

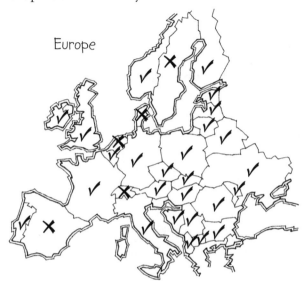

Europe

2. *Why were they fighting?*

(a) No one agrees about this − and no one agreed in 1914 either!

(b) After one country attacked another country (it all kicked off between Serbia and Austria) all their friends wanted to join the party. Serbia's friends were Russia, France and Britain (and all Britain's other friends too − Canada, New Zealand . . .). These were the Allied countries (a very posh name for them). Austria's friends were Germany and Turkey (the country, NOT the bird). These were the Axis powers (another posh title). And when all of these were enjoying the party everyone else wanted to join in too.

(c) Did they need a reason? After a fairly quiet and peaceful hundred years it was high time to have a bit of fun and games, and killing and shooting . . .

3. *What in the world did little Wales have to do with all this?*

(a) Because Wales was part of GREAT Britain in this period, she didn't have much choice.
(b) Not a lot, except that Wales liked prying into every other country's business.
(c) Wales felt very sorry for small countries like Belgium and Serbia and was prepared to challenge the bullies of Germany and Austria.

* When the British wanted to be very spiteful, they called the Germans Huns – beastly barbaric bullies from their ancient history – just like the Saxons in English history!

4. *What did the women do at home in Wicked Wales while the men were away having a good time fighting?*

(a) They went out to steal the men's jobs in the factories and on the farms.

(b) They hid in cupboards until the war was over.

Cooey! Is it safe for me to come out now?

(c) They sat by the fire knitting socks to keep the poor soldiers' feet warm in the terrible trenches.

Answers
1 b + c;
2 b (and a little bit of a + c too);
3 a + c; 4 a + c.

LET'S BEGIN AT THE BEGINNING – HOW TO PERSUADE POOR PEASANTS TO JOIN THE BARMY ARMY!

That was THE question. Fortunately, Wicked Wales had several sleazy star performers who understood the Welsh people well, and who knew how to recruit wide-eyed boys into their barmy army.

STAR PERFORMER 1 *

David Lloyd George
The sleaziest star of all. He was only a poor peasant from Llanystumdwy on the Llŷn peninsula, but he became Prime Minister of Britain between 1916 and 1922. The people of Wales adored this wonderful Welsh wizard. He called upon them to support the little nations – under 5 feet 5 inches (or 1.651 metres to you and me) – of the world. And of course the Welsh swallowed the wizard's words hook, line and sinker.

Serbia 1.600 metres   Belgium 1.640 metres   Wales 1.500 metres

Germany 3.500 metres

STAR PERFORMER 2 ★★

The Reverend John Williams, Brynsiencyn
An important Methodist preacher who wore his army uniform when he preached from the chapel pulpit. He recruited thousands of farm servants from north Wales to join the army – well done, Johnny boy!

STAR PERFORMER 3 ★★★

Brigadier General Owen Thomas

He had fought in the Boer War in South Africa, so at least he knew what it was like to be a soldier. He managed to recruit 4,000 lads from Anglesey alone (there weren't many young men left on the island!). But he and his poor wife Frederica paid a VERY high price for all this war propaganda. They lost three of their four sons, Robert, Owen and Trefor, on the battlefield, and the other son had died already (very, very, very, very sad).

This is the sort of awful advert O.T. would have used to recruit his troops:

YOUNG MEN OF ANGLESEY

Do you want to serve Wales?
(that is – do you want to kill people?)
Join the *Royal Welch Fusiliers*
(can't spell 'Welsh' correctly?)

Age 19-35 Height 167 centimetres
Chest size 90 centimetres

How to join? – Go to your local Police Station

GOD SAVE THE KING (and keep him in England!)

Star Recruiters' Striking Tactics

- **Setting up a Welsh Corps** (great name because most of them would be corpses before long anyway) within the British Army – with Owen Thomas as its Colonel and John Williams as its chaplain (minister). Jobs for the boyos. A very clever idea because now friends from the same area could join up together (and be killed together and at the same time). Bye-bye, all you **lad**s from Llanrhudd-**lad**!

- **Allowing Welsh soldiers to speak Welsh and write home in Welsh.** Big deal! English was the official language of the British Army, because they were afraid that the Welsh were spiteful spies, who would leak secret information in Welsh code to the enemy in their letters home.

In a letter home Furness Williams from Ruthin, who was an excellent singer, said:

Help!

CUNNING CODES

A very important rule for spiteful spies:
DO NOT name the place where you are fighting. This could help the enemy find the British army.

But some Welsh soldiers devised cunning codes. In a letter home one said he liked to '*bwyta afalau*'. You don't get it? Well, his family didn't either! '*Bwyta afalau*' means 'Eat apples' in English – that is, Étaples – a town in France. Don't choke on the joke!

Sam Johnson wrote home from Palestine to his religious parents and said he was near the place where Samson had carried the city gates. Mum and Dad rushed for their Bible and saw that their very dear but cunning son was in Gaza in Palestine.

- **Composing stirring songs** – saying nasty things about the cruel enemy and calling upon the Welsh to enlist for war at once.

  Such stirring songs were said to be **JINGO**ISTIC. Here's one of the favourites. Sing it to the popular tune 'Bing bong and bing bong bay'.

  > Your country needs you. Don't delay,
  > Remember Wales's glorious past,
  > The princes brave who joined the fray:
  > Rhys, Glyndŵr and Llywelyn the Last.★

★ A silly tactic because Lord Rhys had died in bed in 1197 and Llywelyn the Last only lasted until 1282. But some say that Owain Glyndŵr is asleep in a cave somewhere in Wales. Since 1415 he's been waiting for the Welsh to come and shake him awake. Wake up, Glyndŵr – your country needs you NOW!

Chorus:
Jing, jong and jing jong jay . . .

Teach the cruel foe a lesson,
You'll be back before you're missed.
You'll be home in time for Christmas,★★
Come on, boys! Make haste! Enlist.

Chorus:
Jing, jong and jing jong jay . . .

- **Creating propaganda posters** (propaganda is a big word for 'persuading') – they were enough to make you cry – or immediately rush to enlist in the army.

★★ Everyone thought that the war would be over by Christmas 1914! But Christmas 1918 would be nearer the mark. (You can go back to sleep for another four years, Father Christmas.)

PROPAGANDA POSTERS
the Art of
(Mis)information

And one of the most popular songs during the wasteful First World War was written by Ivor Novello, the warm-hearted Welshman from Cardiff. It called upon all brave Welsh mothers and wives to look after their homes while their darling sons and husbands were away at war.

Keep the home fires burning
While your hearts are yearning,
Though your lads are far away
They dream of home;
There's a silver lining
Through the dark clouds shining,
Turn the dark cloud inside out
'Til the lads come home.

- **Using brilliant bullying tactics** – when silly young girls saw men who hadn't joined the army in the street, they ran up to them and gave them a white feather to wear. White was the colour of shame – a coward's colour.

Take that, you contemptible cowardy custard!

Please don't – you're tickling me!

It could be quite handy when a girlfriend wanted to get rid of a boyfriend she'd lost interest in!

- **Winding up the Welsh to make them hate the enemy – especially the Germans**
In Aberystwyth, at the beginning of the war, a crowd attacked the home of a German called Dr Ethé. They were baying for his blood. Dr Ethé was a very clever man and he could speak six languages but he only knew ONE word of Welsh '*cwrw*' (beer)! Perhaps it would have been wiser if he'd learnt a few others such as '*Iechyd da*' (Good health); '*Heddwch*' (Peace) and '*Ewch i ffwrdd!*' (Go away!).

And they even attacked daschunds *(hund* means dog in German) by spitting at them and kicking them!

As a result, by May 1915, 100,000 young Welsh lads had caught the war fever.

And, of course, on the enemy's side, the Germans and Austrians had also been learning jingoistic songs and reading propaganda posters and were hell-bent on killing as many enemy soldiers as possible: English, Scottish, French, Welsh . . .

I DO NOT BELIEVE IT!

It's difficult to believe some of the tedious tales about Wicked Wales and World War 1. What do you think – are they **TRUE** or **FALSE**? YOU decide!

1. Before any man could become a soldier he had to see a doctor. And surprise, surprise – many Welshmen weren't fit enough to go to war. They were too short or their eyesight was poor.

TRUE or **FALSE?**

You're too short, your eyes are weak and your knees are bent.

But I've worked down the coalmine for over ten years!

2. Some young lads were so keen to join the army, they lied about their age. You had to be 18 years old to be a soldier.

TRUE or **FALSE?**

3. After the young men had joined the army they had to learn how to use guns and bayonets, and how to kill. One training camp was in Sunny Rhyl. No wonder the boys thought they were on holiday.

TRUE or **FALSE?**

4. Once the men had joined the Welsh Corps the rest of Wales forgot all about them. Bye-bye and so long, boyos!

TRUE or **FALSE?**

5. Every letter sent from the trenches was read by a man called a censor. His miserable little job was to check that no important war secrets had been leaked in the letters. But, with 12,500,000 letters being posted from France every week there was far too much work for one slow censor.

TRUE or **FALSE?**

6. Welsh coalminers were very useful in the war effort, to dig down under No Man's Land, between the British and enemy lines.

TRUE or **FALSE?**

7. By 1916 far fewer men were willing to come forward to join the army and be killed in battle (what a surprise!). So the government had to pass a law which FORCED men between 18 and 45 years old to enlist as soldiers.

TRUE or **FALSE?**

ANSWERS

1. TRUE But the army was so desperate for men that it decided to accept very small men, under 5 feet 3 inches, into its ranks. The 'bantam battalion' was established for these recruits ('bantams' are tiny hens and cockerels!).

♪ Heigh ho, heigh ho! It's off to war we go.
♪ We're the bantams small, we're one for all,
♪ Heigh ho, heigh ho, heigh ho, heigh ho!

2. TRUE Alfred Wookey from Canton, Cardiff went to the Recruiting Office in August 1915 and claimed he was 19 years old. In fact he was only 14! His parents heard about his white lie, and within six months he had been sent packing back home. (Perhaps being in the army was better than having a clout from his mam!)

3. TRUE And they loved it – for a few months at least. Sunbathing on the sands, riding on the donkeys and eating strawberry (blood-red!) ice cream on the prom. The greatest problem was that the beach in Sunny Rhyl was very different from the terrible trenches in France. And stabbing sandbags with a bayonet was very different from stabbing another man's stomach – SPLOTCH! One of these mollycoddled soldiers said:

> I've been learning to drill for weeks in Colwyn Bay, wearing a bowler hat and carrying the handle of a brush as a gun.

4. FALSE Every member of the Welsh Corps received a copy of a special book, *The Land of My Fathers – a Welsh Gift Book*, as a nice little present to take with them into battle. But how did they feel after reading scintillating stories about 'St David's Death', 'The Baby's Funeral', and 'Dying in a Foreign Land'?! And who organised this pathetic present? Margaret Lloyd George of course. (Does the name ring a bell?)

5. TRUE And if any petty soldier took a photograph of the terrible trenches or the battlefield, he would be shot dead! Intelligent historians (there are some!) have also noticed that there aren't many pictures of dead bodies of British soldiers (in case you wanted one for your bedroom wall!). They said that such pictures would have broken people's hearts, though in most cases their hearts were broken already.

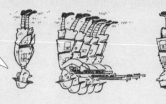

I hope someone is taking a photograph of this for me to send home!

6. TRUE Because they had worked underground for years in coalmines and slate quarries, the Welsh were brilliant at digging tunnels. The piece of land between the trenches was called 'No Man's Land' – an excellent name because the only things there were dead bodies and ordinary soldiers, and they were nobodies, weren't they? The only problem was that the Germans were also digging tunnels to try to place explosives to blow the Brits to bits! The two sides could have met midway!

Halt! Who goes there?

Dai bach y Sowldiwr!

7. TRUE Using force or conscription was very, very unpopular. And the young men began to hide under beds and behind doors to avoid being forced to become brave warriors for Wales.

Just thought I'd save you some time and money!

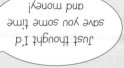

AND HERE WE ARE –
HELL ON EARTH

(OK, OK! We all know that hell is UNDERGROUND – but the trenches were deep.)

Why don't **YOU** relive life in the terrible trenches? Your history teachers would love it, and you would have great marks in the next test. (Of course, they would never be willing to suffer such hardship themselves.)

But where?
You could be sent to fight for the British army all over the world:

 on the Western Front in trenches in France and Belgium. These trenches ran all the way from Switzerland for 440 miles (almost three times the length of Wales) to the North Sea. After one battle, Germany would have gained a mile or two of land; following the next battle, France or Britain would have won this land back. Back and fore, back and fore – no wonder both sides were bemused and confused!

Well I never, we're back where we began yesterday!

on the front between Austria and Italy – in ice-filled trenches rather than muddy ones

 in Macedonia in the Mediterranean, to help Serbia against Germany, Austria-Hungary and Bulgaria

Here is one soldier's description of a major battle in this area in 1918:

It's impossible to describe the bravery of these Welshmen. Because there was gas around we had to wear our breathing apparatus. Just imagine fighting with a hot gas mask on your face, staring through fuzzy goggles and sucking the end of a rubber pipe in your mouth. And in the scorching sun. And firing at the enemy at the same time. One dreadful day the 7th Battalion of the South Wales Borderers lost very many men. The land was covered in a haze when the Borderers attacked. Then, suddenly, the haze evaporated and the soldiers walked into an explosion of bullets from the Bulgarian machine guns. At the end of the day only one officer and 18 men were left alive. You could hear the injured soldiers screaming and crying from the hillsides.

 in Gallipoli, against Turkey *(gobble, gobble!)*

at sea – all across the world. When, in December 1917, a German submarine attacked the *Aragon,* 610 soldiers died. She was on her way to Egypt. The *Attack* rushed to the scene to rescue the men from the sea. They took their clothes off because they were soaking in oil and they put the men to lie naked on deck. THEN a torpedo hit the *Attack.* Everyone was thrown into the sea. Because their bodies were covered in oil the sailors from the *Aragon* couldn't swim. Hundreds more drowned!

 in several other dangerous places, such as Palestine, Egypt and Iraq – all over the world. One soldier from Cynwyl Elfed was frightened by the teeth of the Egyptian camels!

Please file them as sharply as you can to frighten the enemy!

What a woeful World War!

Before going to hell you would need to be fitted with the latest fashionable, official uniform.

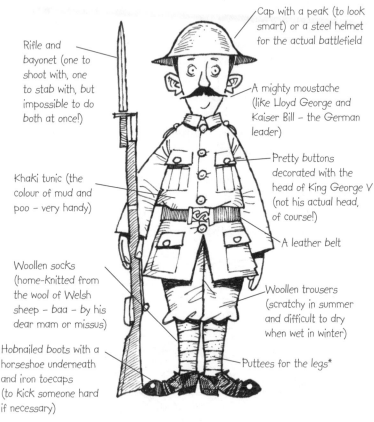

Cap with a peak (to look smart) or a steel helmet for the actual battlefield

Rifle and bayonet (one to shoot with, one to stab with, but impossible to do both at once!)

A mighty moustache (like Lloyd George and Kaiser Bill – the German leader)

Pretty buttons decorated with the head of King George V (not his actual head, of course!)

Khaki tunic (the colour of mud and poo – very handy)

A leather belt

Woollen socks (home-knitted from the wool of Welsh sheep – baa – by his dear mam or missus)

Woollen trousers (scratchy in summer and difficult to dry when wet in winter)

Hobnailed boots with a horseshoe underneath and iron toecaps (to kick someone hard if necessary)

Puttees for the legs*

* To make puttees for your legs you will need:
  – two long pieces of cloth, 2.75 metres long, 75 centimetres wide
  – pieces of sticky tape
  – the patience of a saint!

Wind the pieces of cloth round and round and round your legs from the ankle to the knee and secure with pieces of tape. These puttees were supposed to be good at keeping water, mud and any horrible little insects out of your shoes. But they were useless – if they were too loose, you could stumble over them; but if they were too tight they would stop the blood from circulating to your feet (well, almost). No wonder the soldiers hated them.

I don't think I quite mastered the putees yet!

After marching across France (for mile after mile – keeping to the right side of the road of course!) you would reach the terrible trenches. Then you would have to follow the boring daily routine of a day on the front line.

A QUIET DAY IN THE TERRIBLE TRENCHES

1. About 5 o'clock in the morning, when everything is pitch black: 'Stand-to-Arms' – take up your weapons and stand on the firing step in case the enemy decides to attack at dawn. But the enemy is doing exactly the same thing!

2. At dawn: shoot shells and fire the guns to frighten the enemy out of their wits. And the enemy will be doing exactly the same! This horrid little game was called 'the morning hate'.

Hic!

3. A shot of rum all round (Yum yum. Hic! – drinking on an empty stomach).

...nspect the troops. Many of the officers ... *hach* (toffs) and they look down their ... the Welsh soldiers. They call them ... from the river Taff, probably. The ... nicknames for all the soldiers: ...ummies' from Birmingham, 'Jocks' from Scotland, 'Micks' from Ireland ...

5. Breakfast – at last! No shooting or attacking – and the enemy follows suit. A chance to relax. But the officers aren't happy. They like to send the soldiers out to collect dead bodies from No Man's Land instead.

6. Finishing off the interesting daily tasks – filling sandbags, draining trenches, cleaning toilets – **THE** most miserable and stinking job in the whole world! The best toilets are only 1–2 metres deep, the worst ones are holes made by falling shells. *Ych a fi!* Sometimes the soldiers drink water from these filthy holes without realising they've been used as toilets! *Ych – ych a fi!*

7. A chance to write letters home, or to make pretty little ornaments out of bullet cases to send back to your girlfriend.

8. Sunset and another 'Stand-to-Arms'.

9. In the dark – out onto No Man's Land to mend the barbed wire, collect dead bodies or to try to eavesdrop and overhear important enemy secrets.

TASTY FOOD IN THE TRENCHES

Here is your chance to recreate a fantastic feast from the food rations the soldiers received.

You will need:

- hundreds of tins of corned beef
- very hard dry biscuits (I hope you don't have false teeth)
- tea
- stale bread, full of maggots
- at the beginning of the war perhaps you would be lucky enough to have salt, and blackcurrant jam too

Yum yum or yuk?

It's not surprising that every soldier loved receiving a food parcel from home.

When I eat bread and butter (where did he get butter?), I close my eyes and think of the hills and fields of dear old Wales.

One Welsh soldier decided he'd like some chips to eat, so he grew potatoes in No Man's Land. When they were ready he lit a fire in the dugout and melted some magarine in his helmet (where did he get magarine?) to make chips. But an important officer saw the fire and rushed over. The soldier threw the helmet onto his head and the fat dripped down over his face.

What's wrong with your face, Taff?

My hair's very greasy, sir!

And don't forget the one other ridiculous ration: 566 grams of tobacco.

They're determined to kill us one way or another!

BUT CAN YOU STOMACH THE WHOLE TRUTH?

If you dared to write the whole truth in a letter, it would probably have said something like this. But first you would need to make some invisible ink.

To make invisible ink

You will need:
- water
- an equal amount of baking soda (where would you get hold of baking soda? You'd have to pretend you were going to bake a nice little cake)
- white paper
- a twig

1. Mix the water and the baking soda.
2. Write your message on the paper with the twig and leave it to dry. It will disappear.
3. To read the message hold the paper up to a candle flame or an electric bulb (of course very few homes had electricity in Wales in 1914–1918!). The writing will appear in a brown colour and you'll be able to read it.

O dear, I won't be able to read this letter from the light of my life after all!

~~Somewhere in Belgium~~ (the censor has obviously been very, very busy)

March 1916

Dear Mam,

I hope you are well and have bought a smart new outfit for Easter. It won't be much of an Easter here in the terrible trenches ~~unfortunately. For most of the time we have to hang around waiting, and waiting and waiting for something (anything) to happen and by the time it does our nerves are in shreds. Life is horrible here. I'm up to my knees in cold wet mud the whole time. It's a mud bath – like being in a potato field. But there aren't any potatoes growing in these fields, just the legs and heads of dead men. We live like animals, in holes in the ground. And between the mud and filth, the sweat, the toilets and the dead bodies, the stench is unbearable. I can't remember when I last had a wash.~~

Sometimes we try to break the monotony by singing Welsh songs. Dai from Aberdare has a lovely voice and the Germans enjoy his singing too. They clap and shout encore, so Dai sings 'Land of my Fathers' with gusto. ~~Well, since this is our national anthem we have to stand up for it, even though that means we can be seen over the top of the trench and can be shot dead.~~

He'll be back in the 'land of his fathers' sooner than he thought!

And then, suddenly, bullets whizz past – th–thhh–phudd. The sound phudd comes when a bullet hits some poor soldier's body. The secret snipers are the worst though. Poor old Johnny only peeped over the top of the trench from the firing step and the next minute – phudd – a bullet shot him dead as a dodo (poor dab!). I hope his mother had a letter to tell her he's gone.

What does this letter say, I wonder? I don't understand any English.*

* Twenty per cent of Welsh people didn't understand any English in 1914, and yet the letters sent home to inform families that a soldier had died were all in English!

43

And then the machine guns start – ratt-t-t-t – one bullet after the other with no mercy. The officers have had a strange brainwave – they think it would be a good idea if a large number of soldiers went out of the trenches, over the top, at the same time and try to rush the machine guns. A brainwave? They need to have their heads examined! The machine guns kill one row of soldiers after the other. And if you're fortunate enough to avoid the guns you can get caught in the barbed wire, which is all over No Man's Land. I've seen injured soldiers hanging from the barbed wire, unable to move, and left there to die.

But the huge shells are the worst of all – whizz-bang – exploding and blowing men to bits. A shell blew my best friend to pieces and his skin and flesh stuck to me like red clay for several days (excuse me, I feel sick – ugh-ugh-ugh – when I think about it).

And I mustn't mention the vile vermin which share the trenches, or the other dangerous and horrible things which kill and maim, in case the censor refuses to send this letter to you.

But there's no point complaining. And I have to admit that I'm looking forward very much to pay-back time. I'm going to go out there and kill every bloodthirsty enemy. Ratt-tt-t, whizz-bang, phudd!!!

Soaking and stinking best wishes from your scaredy-cat son,

Madog

Well, if Madog wasn't allowed to mention them, we certainly can:

THE VILE VERMIN IN THE TRENCHES

What were they? Have a guess:

(1) What a nightmare these were for the soldier
As they jumped from one head to the other,
These horrible nits
Sent him out of his wits,
And the itching continued forever.

(2) They look so ferocious and ugly
As they feed on the wounds of the army,
But in fact they're quite sweet
And quite good, 'cos they eat
Rotten flesh, leaving only the healthy!

(3) They lodged in the seams of your breeches
And gnawed like an army of leeches,
So the soldiers would kill
Every one (what a thrill!)
By burning or squeezing the creatures!

(4) On the flesh of the corpses it fed
As it gorged on the blood of the dead.
Each one grew so fat
And as big as a cat,
Till the stench filled the soldiers with dread.

Have you guessed correctly?

ANSWERS

(1) **HEAD LICE** – And these still worry schoolchildren today! But the poor soldiers didn't have a nit comb or a special shampoo to kill them.

No chance, you nitwit!

I'll catch you!

46

(2) **MAGGOTS** – If you ate maggot's eggs (by mistake of course) they could go right through your body and eat your internal organs (and your liver would be particularly tasty). But during the First World War doctors noticed that wounds full of maggots healed more quickly than clean wounds. And today they are bred in laboratories for hospital use. (What clever maggots!)

(3) **BODY LICE** – If the soldiers hadn't washed for six weeks, their clothes would be full of lice, scratching and itching their skins. The soldiers tried to get rid of them, but nothing really worked except a very hot bath and burning all their clothes.

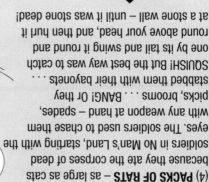

They hid in my pants. I used to burn them with a candle until they squirted out like Chinese crackers! When I had finished, my face was covered in red blood spots! I'll try to kill the rest by squeezing them hard between my thumb and forefinger and splattering them all over the place!

(4) **PACKS OF RATS** – as large as cats because they ate the corpses of dead soldiers in No Man's Land, starting with the eyes. The soldiers used to chase them with any weapon at hand – spades, picks, brooms . . . BANG! Or they stabbed them with their bayonets . . . SQUISH! But the best way was to catch one by its tail and swing it round and round above your head, and then hurl it at a stone wall – until it was stone dead!

Ha ha – this is better than the big wheel on Barry Island.

SPLAT!

47

SCREAM AND SHOUT ... IN HOSPITAL!

If you want a true picture of the dreadful dangers of the terrible trenches you will have to visit a military hospital, full of injured soldiers. So, hold your nose, take a deep breath, keep a handkerchief handy and in you go.

WARD 1

A roomful of soldiers without arms, feet, legs or ... Several of them have trench foot. Because the trenches were so wet and the soldiers' boots were so poor, their feet would swell up to twice their usual size and they wouldn't be able to feel them at all. One soldier describes how he could pierce his foot with a bayonet and feel no pain. The flesh had rotted completely.

Oops! – Oh, no problem!

Treatment:
 (i) After 1915 every soldier was issued with three pairs of socks to wear in the trenches (that put a sock in it!).
(ii) Massage with whale oil (more stench!). The soldiers at the front used ten gallons of whale oil a day.

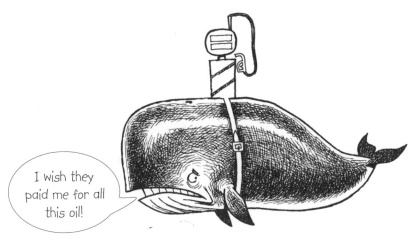

I wish they paid me for all this oil!

Nothing doing?
No choice then, but to chop off the foot. At least you couldn't fight in the trenches ever again.

WARD 2

The patients in this ward have been in contact
with dangerous gases. About 90,000, Russians mostly,
were killed by gases. Every soldier was scared stiff of
a gas attack.

Tear gas made the soldiers cry and sneeze. It was very
painful and it could make them blind. And mustard gas
burned the eyes and caused large blisters
to swell up on the skin and inside the body.

Treatment:
Before there were gas masks you could soak your
sock in your own urine and hold it up to your nose.
Of course it was difficult to fight then, and you could
catch trench foot without your socks!

If you came into contact with gas you could put vinegar from a bottle of pickles on your eyes. Ouch!

But before long all the soldiers, dogs and horses (but not the rats) in the trenches were issued with gas masks (horribly smelly and very ugly rubber masks).

WARD 3

The patients in this ward look awful because they are suffering from SHOCK! Huge shells would explode unexpectedly and give the poor soldiers the shock of their lives. And just seeing all the dead, unburied corpses in No Man's Land would give other soldiers a dreadful shock. They would see the dead faces turning from greyish-yellow, to red, to purple, and then to black, and the stomachs would swell and explode.

These patients would have nightmares and couldn't sleep or eat. Others would shake hysterically and wouldn't be able to control their movements at all.

Treatment:
(i) Tell them to behave like men and not like frightened mice.
(ii) Give the poor patients another, bigger, shocking shock.

(iii) Try any of these treatments: electric shock, hypnosis, massage, rest, discussion, therapy . . . that's better!

Some would get better, but others suffered from shock for the rest of their lives.

WARD 4

There aren't many in this ward because it's for men who have tried to escape from the army by shooting themselves – in the foot, leg, arm . . . But can you blame them?

And if you had visited a military hospital in France, Germany, or in many other parts of the world, you would have seen the same deep despair and the same insufferable suffering.

MERRY CHRISTMAS 1914

Believe it or not, this is a true story. It will lift up your heavy hearts amidst the awesome anguish of the wretched First World War. Welshmen like R. Morris from Flint and E.R. Bowden from Bangor were THERE!

Merry Christmas, *Nadolig Llawen –*
Frohe Weihnachten, **everyone!**

A TRIUMPHANT MOMENT FOR THE WELSH BOYS?

WE MUST TAKE THE TREES - THE BATTLE OF MAMETZ WOOD

Hopeless historians cannot agree. Did the Welsh troops who fought in the battle of Mametz Wood behave bravely? Or was it all a complete catastrophe?

ORDER OR DISORDER?

THAT is the question. YOU decide.

And here are some **Fantastic Facts** to help you to see the wood through the trees:

 The battle of Mametz Wood was part of the gruesome battle of the Somme. During the battle of the Somme about 20,000 soldiers were killed on the first day – 1 July 1916 – and by the time the battle had ended in November about 1,262,000 had been killed or injured on both sides.

 The battle of Mametz Wood took place on 7–12 July and the aim was to capture the largest forest on the banks of the river Somme.

The task of taking the trees fell to the 38th Welsh Division, and other divisions of the army were there to help too.

Prickly Points: "The blame for making a complete mess of things rests firmly on the shameful shoulders of the Generals."

The Generals were about six miles behind the front line! And apparently they couldn't even read a map!

They decided to order their soldiers to advance in rows across open meadowland where there was no shelter at all – and where the German machine guns – in front of them and to their side – could pick them out easily (very *twp* tactics).

The British shells were being fired from behind their front line and they landed on the Welsh soldiers themselves!

Because of the total shambles during the first day of battle the leader of the 38th Division, Lieutenant Ivor Philipps from Pembrokeshire, was told to pack up and go home with his tail between his legs. But those who replaced him weren't much better either.

Prickly Points: "The blame for creating complete chaos lies squarely with the Welsh soldiers."

 According to Siegfried Sassoon, a popular poet (was he English or German?), the Welsh were tiny men who behaved like a 'gang of toddlers'. (Do you need large men to fight through a wood then?)

Many of the men had lost faith in the war effort. (What a surprise after almost two years of fighting!)

 Many of the soldiers of the 38th Division had not received sufficient military training before being sent out to France. (Whose fault was that?)

The men became entangled in the trees. It was very difficult to fight in a wood full of tree trunks. Those that did manage to get to the wood had to fight with bayonets and it was difficult to know who was who. In the panic some Welshmen were killed by their own men! This was called 'friendly fire'! (With friends like these, who needs enemies?!)

Final Score

A DRAW, 4 points each.

But here are a few further **Frantic Facts**
to consider:

Who won the battle? The British Army of
course — thanks to the Welsh effort. By 12 July
they had taken the trees.

Almost 4,000 men of the 38th Welsh Division
sacrificed their lives in this brutal battle. Among
them there were three sets of brothers. Tom and
Henry Hartwidge from Ferndale fought side by side.
Tom was shot in the head and Henry rushed to help
him and was shot too. Tom had a wife and three children,
and Henry a wife and one child (yes, very sad indeed).

And today an iron sculpture — a grand Welsh dragon —
stands proudly in Mametz Wood to commemorate the
Welsh troops who won the wood for Britain.

Here I stand in this field
of poppies*,
To prove to the WORLD
that the Welsh were not babies.

* Everyone knows that the red poppy is the sobering symbol of the
First World War. They are sold for Remembrance Sunday in November
every year, to raise money to help soldiers who have been injured in wars.

In memory of the Battle of Mametz Wood we can sing this little song:

Under the weeping hazel tree
The soldiers marched – to victory?
Sent into battle by their bosses,
The soldiers suffered dreadful losses.

PATHETIC PORTRAIT
OF A HAPLESS HERO

Every school child in Wicked Wales (and in THE
WHOLE WIDE WORLD) should know the horrible
history of this hapless hero, Hedd Wyn, or that's what
your history teachers probably believe. They love this
sentimental story and they like repeating it over and
over again (yawn, yawn!). And to help them – here it is
once more! Now swallow it whole and then you can
claim to be a full-blooded Welsh patriot.

Name: Ellis Humphrey Evans (his bardic name
Hedd Wyn means 'Blessed Peace' –
a strange name considering his
unfortunate history!)

Home: Yr Ysgwrn, Trawsfynydd, north Wales
(a small farm far, far away from the fields
of Flanders)

Work: a shepherd (but he daydreamed
all the time and the sheep roamed far and wide)

History: In 1916 his brother Robert, who had just got
married, was conscripted (forced to join up) into the
army, but Ellis offered to go instead of him (a truly
heroic hero). In June 1917 he was sent to join the Royal
Welch Fusiliers in France and on 15 July he was about to
join the great battle in Passchendaele, Flanders. He said
he had never seen such a beautiful country (but do
remember that he was a romantic poet).

Hobbies:
(i) Chasing girls (why not?)
(ii) Composing poetry and winning competitions in eisteddfodau (very cool in 1917). He came second in the competition for the bardic chair at the Aberystwyth National Eisteddfod in 1916. When he was home on the farm in 1917 he composed a poem on the subject *Yr Arwr* (The Hero) to compete for the chair at the Birkenhead National Eisteddfod. He finished the poem but didn't have a chance to post it (just imagine! — this story could have been completely different). Then, on his way to France he redrafted it and posted it on 15 July.

The end: At 3.50 in the morning on 31 July, in torrential rain and with the battlefield awash with mud, Hedd Wyn's battalion tried to capture Pilkhem Ridge. At 5.00 Hedd Wyn was hit by a shell; but he was left to lie on the battlefield for hours, waiting for the medical team to carry him to hospital.

Hedd Wyn died at 11.00. He asked the poor doctor a very difficult question, and these were his last words:

Hedd Wyn fought on the battlefield for only just over an hour! How tragic!

BUT: The really important story (as everyone knows) is that Hedd Wyn's brilliant poem, under the French pen name Fleur de Lis, WON the chair at the Birkenhead National Eisteddfod (but unfortunately he wouldn't have much use for a chair now). Dyfed, the Archdruid, called out the pen name, the two great trumpets sounded out, but no poet got up to claim the chair. Dyfed explained the sad saga and a black cloth was thrown over the chair. There were enough tears in the pavilion to match the incessant rain on the faraway fields of Flanders.

The people of Wales will remember this sobering story for ever and ever . . .

(Too true – schoolchildren are still being plagued with the tale today.)

In memoriam:

- there is a statue of Hedd Wyn (as a shepherd, not a soldier) in Trawsfynydd;
- you can see the Black Chair in Yr Ysgwrn;
- another famous Welsh bard wrote a brilliant poem in his memory (learn it by heart if you want to make a great impression on your Welsh teachers). Here we go: 'Y bardd trwm dan bridd tramor . . .' ('In foreign soil the poet grave . . .');
- AND in 1992 a fantastic film about him was nominated for an OSCAR. Unfortunately, it didn't win!

OH, YES – HEDD WYN was the hapless hero of Wales during the wasteful First World War.

This hero gets 10/10!

CRIME AND PUNISHMENT DURING THE WASTEFUL FIRST WORLD WAR

Would you like to be shot by your own troops? This was easy enough during the First World War because the army had so many stupid rules.

If an ordinary soldier broke any rule he could be summoned before a Military Tribunal – lots of crabby, heartless (well, they didn't show they had hearts anyway!) old men, sitting behind a huge table and deciding how to punish tragic offenders as cruelly as possible.

YOU can be the bumptious Chair of this Military Tribunal and decide which penalty fits which crime in this table. And remember – NO MERCY!

A TABLE OF TRAGIC OFFENCES AND THEIR PAINFUL PUNISHMENTS

TRAGIC OFFENCES	PAINFUL PUNISHMENTS
1. Shooting a pigeon on its way home*	A. Shot dead
2. Shooting a British soldier when drunk	B. A fine of £100 or 6 months imprisonment
3. Spying for the enemy	C. Shot dead
4. Sleeping when on duty in the trenches	D. Sent straight to fight at the Front
5. Photographing the trenches	E. Shot dead
6. Late arriving back from a home visit	F. Shot dead

* Pigeons and dogs were the soldiers' best friends – the dogs carried messages quickly from the trenches to the army generals who were usually as far away from the battlefield as they could possibly be.

Not much choice, was there? Shooting (and wasting bullets) was the favourite punishment – for every offence, large or small. It was a dog's life.

And the very clever pigeons? 100,000 of them were used to carry news from the front in France back across the Channel to Britain. They were brilliant at avoiding enemy bullets and 95% of them reached their destinations safely.

NOBODY GIVES A DAMN!

Other soldiers were shot dead by their fellow soldiers –
for deserting or running away from the battlefield. Can
you blame the poor things? During the Wasteful War
360 such soldiers were shot – at least 13 of them from
Wicked Wales.

This is how a newspaper might report such a
horrendous story:

THE CARDIFF ECHO   6 January 1917   6d

DISHONOUR AT THE FRONT

SHOT AT DAWN!

*List of the war dead
pp. 5–20
Winners of the 'spot the
pigeon' competition p. 3*

At 7.30 in the morning
on the 5 January,
the desperate deserter
Edwin Dyett, of Albany
Road, Cardiff, was shot
dead in a farmyard in
France. He had refused to
follow a command to go and
fight on the front line in the
Battle of the Somme.

We asked General Gough for the background to this sad story:

'Well, in the first place, I don't think Dyett was fit to be a lieutenant in the great British Army. Men like him give the Army a bad name. He behaved disgracefully.'

Gough explained what had happened:

'On 3 November when Dyett had lost touch with his unit somewhere on the Somme, another lieutenant ordered him to lead a troop of men back to the front line. But Dyett thought he was too important to follow the orders of a minor lieutenant, and he refused to budge. Instead, he returned to his headquarters. BUT on the way back he claimed he "got lost" (very handy), in thick fog and he was "lost" for two whole days.

After the battle he was reported by the lieutenant and brought before a Court Martial in France.

I've no idea how to get to the Front.

The verdict was that, as a cowardly deserter, he should be shot at dawn, and quite right too. What a splendid warning to every other coward! We'll catch them all and they WILL be punished.'

Unfortunately we can't hear Dyett's version of the story because he's dead. But chaplain Hugh Hughes was with him during his last tragic hours. He said, 'My job is to look after dying men or those about to be shot. It isn't an easy job. I often think that these poor lads don't receive fair play.

Dyett wasn't allowed to see a doctor during the court case and he was probably very, very stressed, poor thing.

He didn't have anyone to defend him in court. And he wasn't allowed to appeal against the verdict either. No, I don't think Dyett was treated fairly at all.'

In the morning, before the shooting, the chaplain was with Dyett. 'I had to lead him out to be shot at dawn. I had to put the mask over his eyes and pin the white poppy on his chest so that the other soldiers could aim accurately at his heart,' Hughes added.

The firing squad was made up of men from Dyett's own unit. One member told us he was shaking and that he couldn't aim straight. One soldier in the squad had a dud bullet in his gun and each one hoped that he was the one.

Mr Dyett, the disastrous deserter's father, didn't have much to say when we called at his home in Albany Road, Cardiff. 'He was only 21 years old,

I think I feel worse than he does! BANG!

poor thing. Did you know that he had written home to his mam the night before being shot, to apologise for bringing shame on the family name? No, I'm sure you didn't. Well, I've had a gutsful of Britain. I've torn up my British passport and I'm going to live in America.' And with that he slammed the door on our jittery journalist!

Well, the *Cardiff Echo* asks – Do we want the fathers of cowardy-custard soldiers living in Wales? Are we glad a disastrous deserter has been shot? Does anyone care?

CONSCIENTIOUS CONCHIES

Some men refused to help the war effort at all:

- because they were Christians and they didn't believe in killing others (excellent);
- because they believed the war had been started by rich people so that they would become richer and more powerful, but that the fighting and suffering would be done by ordinary people, all over the world.

These conscientious objectors (or conchies to everyone except your fussy history teachers), would be brought before the Military Courts to explain why they objected to fighting.

Take the case of Joshua Davies of Lampeter:

Chairman of the Court: Do you use a gun?
Joshua Davies: Yes, to frighten crows.

Chairman: Do you kill rabbits?
JD: Yes, I do.

Chairman: Why aren't you willing to kill Germans then?
JD: I eat rabbits but I don't eat Germans!

Chairman: For such a cheeky answer you will go to prison for two years.
JD: Wow! Thanks a bunch, sir.

The odd (very odd!) chairman sympathised a little (a teensy-weensy bit) with the odd conscientious objector.

Ithel Davies from Mallwyd had a very hard time as a conchie in prison because he refused to do anything at all to help the war effort:

- the prison guard hit him on his nose with a spade until the place was awash with blood, and his nose (not the spade) was broken;
- he was tied into a straightjacket; he couldn't move or bend for six hours.

PRISONERS FROM ALL OVER THE WORLD

Thousands upon thousands of men spent the First World War in prison. Prisoners from Britain in German, Turkish and Italian prisons ... and Germans in prisons in Britain, France ...

Was it safer in prison than on the battlefield, we wonder? Here are two terrifying tales:

1. YOZGAD, TURKEY

A sneaky peek at the diary of Elias Henry Jones from Aberystwyth:

1915
We've arrived at last, after walking 700 miles from Kut-el-Amara to Yozgad (why don't the Turks have sensible names for their towns like Pontrhydfendigaid?). One in seven died on the march. It will be impossible to ESCAPE from here – it's an endless wilderness with mighty mountains surrounding us on all sides.

May 1916
They've tried all sorts of things to turn this prison into a pleasant little place. Today I attended a French lesson (in case I land in a prison in France!) and tomorrow I have a maths lesson (very handy to help me count the grains of rice for supper!). I've also had cookery lessons (cooking snakes) and now they want me to join the orchestra – to play the pipe! It's worse than being in school! AND I WANT TO ESCAPE!

December 1916
An Australian called Hill and I have thought up a brilliant plan to ESCAPE from here. We've persuaded the other prisoners and the prison staff that we can communicate with spirits . . .

and that the spirits have told us where a huge treasure trove has been hidden on the shores of the Mediterranean Sea. We hope they'll want the treasure so much that they will take us to the seashore. And then we can ESCAPE! The 'spirit' talks to me in Welsh nursery rhymes, funnily enough!

Is there anyone there, Jones? Is there anyone there?

'Ifan bach a minne yn mynd i ddŵr y môr' (Ifan bach and I going to the seaside). Yes, the treasure is definitely by the sea.

October 1917
We've decided to try another plan. Hill and I are going to pretend to be completely mad so that we'll be moved to a hospital and then we can ESCAPE. Ga-a-a . . . ga-a-a.

Early October 1918
We need to do something dramatic to prove we're mad. Hill is pretending that he's crazy about the Bible! (There are lots of similar people in Wales.) And I'm going to pretend to hang myself. Ugh-ugh-ugh! I hope I don't succeed. Arghhh!

Hurry up, boyo. Don't hang about!

At the end of October 1918
In Istanbul hospital! I nearly succeeded in hanging myself and spoiling everything! But we have ESCAPED. HOORAY!

1 November 1918
Home at last! It was well worth the effort.

11 November 1918
The war has ended and all the other prisoners are on their way home too! I'm gutted!

After the war Elias H. Jones wrote a book about this tantalising tale and he sold thousands upon thousands of copies of it (no surprise at all!).

2. AN EXCITING ESCAPE FROM DYFFRYN ALED

At the beginning of the war, Dyffryn Aled Mansion in Llansannan was used as a prison for the top brass of the German army. But three of them, Hermann Tholens, Bon Henning and Wolf-Dietrich, ESCAPED. This is Hermann's version of the escapade:

> We had arranged that a German submarine would collect us from Llandudno beach one evening between 13 and 15 August. We managed to ESCAPE from the Mansion and walk to Llandudno. When twilight came we went down to the beach. But there was no sign of the ship – and it didn't appear on the next two evenings either. It seems we were on the wrong beach! By the third day we'd had a gutsful (of waiting, not of food!) and I decided to go and buy some cigarettes. BIG mistake! The shopkeeper noticed that I had a strange accent. He called the police and before nightfall the three of us were back in prison!
> *Ich bin ein Idiot!*

ON THE HOME FRONT IN WALES DURING THE WASTEFUL FIRST WORLD WAR

The Great War was a Soldiers' War. But what about those at home? What did they do for four long years? Watch TV? Have a ball (fun not football!)? What do you think?

There will be much more to say about the home front when we come to the horrendous history of the Second World War. But we must mention the women and the coalminers here too.

THE WONDERFUL WOMEN OF THE FIRST WORLD WAR

During the wasteful First World War many women were given a chance to try new things and to be adventurous.

Do you fancy joining the Land Army?

If so, you must enjoy:

 working long hours – about 48 hours a week

 working outside in all weathers – snow, rain, storms, thunder and lightning . . .

 very hard work – milking crazy cows, shovelling dung, harvesting potatoes, setting traps to catch vermin like moles, rabbits and rats, cutting back thistles without any gloves (ouch!) . . .

being paid very little – the mean old farmers will only pay you a shilling a week (5 pence in today's money), plus food and lodging

 going to a training camp – some were sent to St Fagan's (before it became a museum, of course), to learn what a farm was, and what a cow and a pig looked like ...

Well, I never, so that's where milk comes from!

 listening to fussy farmers moaning about you and saying that women aren't fit to work on farms. (Excuse me, sir, but what about your wife and daughters? They've been at it for years!)

 wearing an ugly uniform which itches and scratches ... (scratch ... itch!)

If you enjoy all that, you are the right woman for this joyless job!

Would you like to work in a factory making explosives or shells?

If so, you must enjoy:

 the company of lots and lots of people, especially women. Of the 10,000 workers at the Munitions Factory in Pembrey 8,000 were women.

 making munitions to kill enemy soldiers. Some girls wrote their names on the shells and gave them a kiss before packing them, to bring them luck, they said – but they weren't very lucky for the poor soldiers they blew up, of course!!

Bye-bye, dear shell – do your best for your country!

 having a woman policeman searching your clothes for cigarettes and matches every morning

No, I haven't got any cigarettes, honestly!

having plenty of money to buy make-up, silk stockings, and a fur coat (WOW!)

 having only half the pay the men had, for exactly the same work (STRIKE NOW!)

 having bright-yellow skin and hair – like a canary – from the sulphur in the explosives. Between 1916 and 1918, 100 girls died of the yellow sickness.

I'm singing like a canary.

I said you look like a canary, not sing like one.

 being in great danger all the time. In the Munitions Factory at Queensferry between 1917 and 1918:
- 3,818 suffered acid burns
- 2,128 had eye injuries
- 763 had skin diseases
- and there were 12,778 other accidents – what an excellent health and safety record! Are you good at maths? If there were 7,000 workers in the Queensferry plant then these would have had 2-3 injuries each a year!

being killed in an explosion.

Here lie

MILDRED OWEN
18 years old

and **DOROTHY WILSON**
19 years old

from Swansea
Killed in Pembrey
Munitions Factory (probably)
August 1917

We're two yellow canaries who made TNT,
We hope that you'll listen, take heed of our plea:
*Don't work in munitions for **our** war is ended,*
We were blown up sky-high, then to heaven we ascended,
But not in the way our Creator intended!

SO, WHO WORE THE TROUSERS?

The women and the girls of course! The men were too busy fighting! And the women filled their trousers (not literally of course) and filled the men's jobs too – as bus and train conductors and drivers, postmen (postwomen!), in the Land Army, in factories and even in the armed services.

Yes, a new world had dawned for women (or so they said!).

HOME COMFORTS

And miserable old women were happy to help the war effort too. Margaret Lloyd George organised a flag day on St David's Day in 1917, and she raised enough money to pay for 60,000 pairs of socks, 14,000 bars of soap and 500,000 cigarettes for the Welsh troops.

Cool Coalminers

Welsh coal was very important as fuel for the Navy during the Great War. But the cool coalminers complained that they weren't being paid enough, while the coal owners were getting richer and richer. The members of the South Wales Miners' **Fed**eration were FED UP! In July 1915 they decided to go on strike. Everyone, especially Bonar Law, the tiresome Tory leader, was very angry with them.

Who won? The miners, of course! They had a pay rise – Welsh coal was much more important than boring Bonar Law.

AND THAT WAS THE END OF THE GREAT WAR

(but there'll be another one soon – so cheer up!)

Some **Foul Facts** about the effects of the war:

They're still discovering 300 tons of shells every year in the fields of Flanders and France.

They're still finding bodies too. In 1992 they came across the body of Thomas John Jenkins (Jac Siencyn to his mam and dad who have long since died) from Pontrhydfendigaid. He had died on the same day as Hedd Wyn (31 July 1917, as you probably recall), in the battle of Passchendaele.

 There are huge cemeteries to remember the soldiers who fought on both sides. In Thiepval are recorded the names of 72,000 soldiers who 'were lost' during the battle of the Somme. These soldiers could fill all the seats in the Millennium Stadium! And in the book which commemorates all those buried at the Menin Gate Cemetery in Belgium there are 20 pages of Joneses!

 Thousands of visitors flock to learn more about the hideous history of the Great War. Every year 300,000 tourists visit Ieper. (But YOU can avoid this frightful fate if you read this brilliant book about the wasteful First World War!)

FROM WAR TO WAR

Not quite, because, between the two World Wars, Wales suffered 20 years of sheer misery and depression.

A TIMELY TIMELINE

1918–19

A flu epidemic kills about 50,000,000 people across the world – more than were killed by the war. The first to die were the young and healthy! All the businesses and schools in Cardiff closed. (Hooray!)

He managed to live through the war in spite of the stench of the trenches, and then he comes home to die of flu in a clean bed in dear old Wales!

1922

Ifan ab Owen Edwards establishes Urdd Gobaith Cymru.
Hey, Mister Urdd, why are you still torturing children
today with your singing, reciting and disco dancing?

1926

The General Strike – everyone on strike for ten days,
but the courageous coalminers carry on for a further
six months.

1929–36

Dreadful depression, unemployment and misery – lots and lots of Welsh people out of work.

1933

Adolf Hitler and the Nazis gain control in Germany. They make the lives of all Jews and gypsies hell on earth.

1934

An appalling accident at Gresford coalmine, near Wrexham. Explosions, gas leaks and fires kill 266 miners.

1936

Three members of Plaid Cymru stage an arson attack on Penyberth farmhouse, on the Llŷn peninsula. They want to stop the government from building a school to train pilots how to bomb other countries. But they are sent to prison. According to one story, D.J. Williams, one of the three hopeless heroes, almost forgot his box of England's Glory matches!

And now we're ready for another World War,
with much more fighting and killing.
(WHOOPEE!)

TO BATTLE! TO ARMS!

THE SAD SECOND WORLD WAR

Yet Another Introduction!

A TEDIOUS TIMELINE

1939
1 September
Germany occupies Poland, starting the Second World War.

1940
10 May
Winston Churchill becomes Prime Minister of Britain and says, 'I have nothing to offer but blood, toil, sweat and tears' (very nice!), and of course the British people (not Churchill) would be the ones having to do most of the bleeding, toiling, sweating and crying!

May–June
The British Army driven out of Europe and fleeing from Dunkirk in France across the sea to Britain – 338,226 British and French soldiers on 850 small boats and ships. But as Saint Winston says, 'We will NOT surrender!'

Au revoir. We're not surrendering, honestly, just going back to fetch better guns, tanks and . . . We'll be back in four years' time!

BRITAIN FRANCE

Summer–Autumn
The Battle of Britain – the German air force, the *Luftwaffe*, attacks Britain incessantly. Britain retaliates by bombing German towns and cities.

1941

January and February
Heavy German bombing air raids during the BLITZ on Cardiff, Swansea and other targets.

June
Germany attacks the Soviet Union.

7 December
Japan attacks the USA navy in Pearl Harbour, Hawaii. America joins the war – high time too!

11 December

Germany and Italy declare war on the USA.

1942

January

The Nazis decide to exterminate all Jews.

May

The Soviet army begins to drive back the German army, and the USA bombs the Japanese fleet. Is the tide turning against Germany?

4 November

Britain defeats the German tanks in the battle of El Alamein in Africa. (What are they doing there anyway?)

1943

February

The Soviet army defeats the Germans in Stalingrad and begins its march on Europe! (Help!)

17 May

The British air force destroys water reservoirs in Germany with its new bouncing bomb – the Dambuster. What fun!

July

The British and American air forces bomb Hamburg in Germany, killing 50,000 people.

The Allied army (i.e. everyone except those supporting Hitler) attacks Italy. Mussolini, the Italian leader, gets the sack!

1944

April onwards

The Soviet army reaches Poland and Romania.

I don't know which is worse – Hitler and the Nazis or Stalin and the Soviets! Help!

The USA approaches Japan and the Allied army penetrates through Italy into Germany. BUT there's still a long way to go.

6 June
D-Day. The Allied army lands in Normandy, France.

1945
27 January
The Soviet army arrives at the atrocious concentration camp in Auschwitz – and the whole world learns about the Nazis' inhuman cruelty against the Jews and anyone else who stood in their woeful way. Emily Bond, a nurse from Swansea, was one of the first to enter the concentration camp at Berben-Belsen. She had to look after 1,000 patients and write down the names of those who died every day.

28 April

Mussolini is executed by shooting and hanging him upside down.

30 April

Hitler kills himself in Berlin after first poisoning his dog, Blondi, and shooting dead his new wife, Eva.

8 May

The war in Europe is over.

6 and 9 August

The USA drops two atomic bombs – on Hiroshima and Nagasaki in Japan, killing around a quarter of a million people in an instant.

15 August

The war against Japan is over.

Great celebrations between May and August – concerts, thanksgiving services, dancing and singing, church bells ringing and street parties galore.

Have another chocolate, *bach* – there'll be plenty of sweets now!

(What a lie! There weren't many sweets around until 1953 – eight years after the war had ended!)

Yes, the sad Second WORLD War was a war between the GREAT world powers. But little Wales played her part too. Welsh soldiers, airmen and sailors fought all over the world in the Army, the RAF and the Navy and they were killed, maimed and imprisoned, just like the soldiers of every other country. Recounting the whole story would bore you stiff, and give you nasty nightmares for the rest of your life.

So, we'll just concentrate on some of the stories about what woeful little Wales and some wonderful Welsh people did to help the GREAT war effort during the sad Second World War.

A GALLERY OF INCREDIBLE ICONS

Here's your chance to prove to your hopeless history teachers (yes, the teachers!) that YOU know more than they do about Wicked Wales and the Welsh people's exceptional exploits during the Second World War. Take them around this gallery and give them a mark out of ten if they've heard of these incredible icons.

A. Taffy Bowen (or Edward George Bowen to his mam and dad) from Swansea. This fantastic physicist helped to develop RADAR – in order to find German aeroplanes at night and enemy submarines down in the deep blue sea. He also discovered how to put radar in bombers. In May 1941 a hundred enemy planes were shot down at night – thanks to radar. This work was very, very important and helped Britain win the Battle of the Atlantic (tremendous work, Taffy!).

MARKS 9/10 (a high score because radar is still very useful today).

B. Wynford Vaughan-Thomas (Wynf to his best friends!) from Swansea (once again!) – an important BBC correspondent who flew with the British bombers over Germany to describe their daring bombing raids.

Here he is at his job:

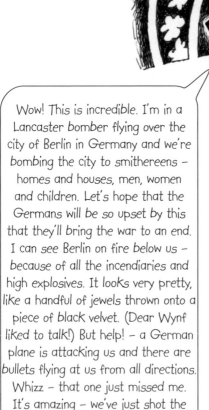

Wow! This is incredible. I'm in a Lancaster bomber flying over the city of Berlin in Germany and we're bombing the city to smithereens – homes and houses, men, women and children. Let's hope that the Germans will be so upset by this that they'll bring the war to an end. I can see Berlin on fire below us – because of all the incendiaries and high explosives. It looks very pretty, like a handful of jewels thrown onto a piece of black velvet. (Dear Wynf liked to talk!) But help! – a German plane is attacking us and there are bullets flying at us from all directions. Whizz – that one just missed me. It's amazing – we've just shot the aeroplane down and it's falling like a flaming oily cloth straight into the middle of the inferno in Berlin.

(An unfortunate little footnote: In 1943–1944, 4,000 people were killed, 10,000 were injured and 450,000 were left homeless in Berlin. But the awesome air raid didn't bring the war to an end – Germany did not surrender and the war went on . . . and on . . . and on.)

MARKS: 7/10

C. Glyndwr Michael – the corpse in the 'Mincemeat Campaign'

Unfortunately poor old Glyndwr had no idea that he had helped the war effort. And the whole campaign was VERY, VERY secret. So – close your eyes when you're reading this sorry story and don't tell ANYONE about it – or you will have to be exterminated!

And that's what happened. Glyndwr Michael was re-named Major William Martin, and the Germans swallowed the 'mincemeat' (the very strange code-name given to this campaign!) hook, line and sinker! After reading the important papers and studying the map, Hitler sent a message to his army in Italy, in secret code of course!

S.O.S.
MOVE THE SOLDIERS FROM SICILY TO SARDINIA AT ONCE! STOP!

And that's how the Allies began to gain territory in Italy – thanks to the dead body of Glyndwr of Aberbargoed.

Deadly MARKS: 10/10

D. Nant-y-gro Reservoir

Your teachers will definitely not have heard this strange story. It was on this unremarkable reservoir in Powys that scientists began testing an enormous bomb capable of blasting a hole in the wall of a dam. This was the famous DAMBUSTER which had to be able to jump and bounce over the water before blowing the dam to bits. (Britain wanted to bomb reservoirs in the Ruhr valley to drown Germany's munitions factories.)

(Another unfortunate little footnote – although the bouncing bomb worked well on the Ruhr, 53 of the British bombing crew were killed and 1,300 local people, including Ukrainian prisoners of war [poor things]!)

MARKS 8/10

E. The Frightening Rhyd-y-mwyn Factory

This was one of the really secret secrets of the Second World War. Here, in a frightening factory, deep in the earth's bowels near Mold, workers were making shells for bombs to carry chemical poisons like mustard gas. Churchill warned the Germans:

If you dare to use chemical gas against us, we'll get you back by doing the same to you. So there!

Fortunately the enemy believed Churchill. But, thanks to the frightening factory at Rhyd-y-mwyn, Britain was all prepared – just in case.

Also (and this was absolutely hush–hush!) it seems that some of the scientists at Rhyd-y-mwyn were working on an atomic bomb – the wickedest war weapon of them all.

MARKS 9/10

F. The End of the World on Mynydd Epynt

Your tedious teachers probably go on and on and on at you about the drowning of Cwm Tryweryn near Bala in the 1950s and 1960s. But everyone should know the sad story of Mynydd Epynt too.

In 1940, the Government stole 30,000 acres of land on Mynydd Epynt to practise shooting and bombing. A school and a chapel were demolished, 54 farms were destroyed and 219 Welsh-speakers were moved from the area. For them this was 'the end of the world'. The Welsh language was killed overnight in this part of Wales. Ffynnon Dafydd Bifan (Dafydd Bevan's well) became Dixie Corner and Tafarn y Mynydd (the Mountain Tavern) became Piccadilly Circus!

I do hope you're in floods of tears by now, and that you will NEVER forget this sad story.

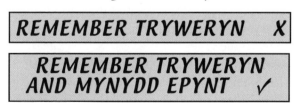

MARKS 8/10

G. The Silent Village – Cruel Revenge

This story is almost too sad to tell. In June 1942, an important Nazi, Reinhard Heydrich, was killed by members of a movement which opposed the Nazis in Czechoslovakia. Hitler was furious when he heard, and ordered that everyone who had helped this movement should be punished severely. The small coalmining village of Lidice was singled out for revenge and, to calm Hitler's terrible temper, every man over 16 years old was executed there and then – 192 of them altogether.

Then they gathered all the women together and sent them to Ravensbrück concentration camp to die.

And what of the children? Their story is also a very, very sad one. They were separated from their mothers – some starved to death and others were sent to the gas chambers to die.

But what has this tragic tale to do with Wales?

In 1943, Humphrey Jennings decided to make a film, *The Silent Village*, to tell the world the story of this evil massacre.

He chose to film it in the coalmining village of Cwmgïedd, near Ystradgynlais, and he used ordinary miners and their families as his actors.

This is how a small village in Wales became part of the effort to prove to the world that Hitler and the Nazis were very cruel.

MARKS 10/10 – full marks for effort.

H. Where are the Hidden Treasures?

Where indeed? That's the question every picture thief was asking during the Second World War. The precious pictures in the Tate Gallery and the National Gallery had disappeared! Who had hidden them and where were they? Where better than Manod slate quarry in Blaenau Ffestiniog? No one would dream of looking down the endlessly long and dark tunnels for beautiful pictures by Rembrandt, Leonardo da Vinci, Renoir and Constable (the police should have looked after every Constable!). And, of course, there weren't any picture thieves in Blaenau Ffestiniog, were there?

MARKS 7/10

Now score your teachers:

50–67 MARKS
Terrific teachers, you should worship the ground they walk on.

25–50 MARKS
OK, but there's room for improvement (as they're always telling you!).

0–25 MARKS
As we thought, they're terrible teachers. You know more than they do!

FLAMING SWANSEA!

That's what the people of Cardiff would have said when they heard that the Germans had dropped more bombs on Swansea than on Cardiff. Swansea and Cardiff have always been rabid rivals – in rugby and football, in shops and theatres ... BUT in the horrific history of the Second World War Swansea came top of the league:

People killed:
1939–1945
Cardiff 355
Swansea 387

And, in February 1941, Swansea suffered the worst blitz in Welsh history.

This is how a jittery journalist would have kept notes on the three nerve-racking nights of the great Swansea blitz.

Wednesday, 19 February

A clear night, full of snow. The Luftwaffe aeroplanes follow the fire in the oil refinery at Llandarcy and the glimmering river Tawe to find their way to Swansea. They are attracted here by the docks and the metal works: 61 planes drop 492 bombs and 15,720 incendiaries on the town. The houses melt away like hot butter. Many people are out watching the show; others are in the cinema. A young policeman has a terrifying experience. A piece of burning phosphorus squirts into his mouth and down his throat. White flames pour out of him – and he dies. The great ack-ack guns try to shoot the enemy planes down. The air raid ends at midnight but everyone is too scared to go to bed.

Thursday, 20 February

The jewellery shop in Wind Street has been bombed – people are on their hands and knees in the rubble searching for precious jewels!

Indeed to goodness, one person's tragedy is another's lucky dip!

The market is hit by a bomb (no more cockles and laver bread for a while then!). An unexploded bomb kills six of the bomb-disposal team. Then, another blitz: the large Wesleyan chapel receives a direct hit and all those sheltering in the cellar are killed instantly. In Teilo Street, three generations of the same family are killed. Glass sparkling everywhere on the streets. The air raid stops at 1 o'clock in the morning.

Friday, 20 February

Another spectacular air raid lasting 5 hours. Gas pipes broken and gas leaking everywhere. Kilvey Hill is lit up like a Christmas tree by the incendiaries. In Wind Street, a man tries to put out an incendiary by stamping on it. His leg is blown away! St Mary's Church suffers a direct hit and the bells ring out wildly as they fall from the tower to the ground. Swansea town centre is burned to the ground and the Grammar School on Mount Pleasant (a rather unfortunate name – Mount Unpleasant would be much more accurate!) is destroyed completely. Everyone's shaken to the core and exhausted by one sleepless night after another.

109

SPECTACULAR STATISTICS ABOUT THE SWANSEA BLITZ

- 56,000 incendiaries and 1,273 bombs dropped on the town.

- Roads, sewerage systems and electricity cables damaged.

- 15 schools destroyed (Hooray! or Oh no!?).

- 6,500 homeless.

- About 230 killed and 409 injured.

- 171 grocer's shops and 34 hotels gutted.

- The popular shop Ben Evans, St Mary's Church and the old market bombed and then demolished.

The whole sky brilliant red. People from Dunvant to Fishguard could see and smell the town burning. Flaming Swansea was AFLAME!

FAIR PLAY TO CARDIFF

We'd better not ignore the bombing of Cardiff, fair's fair. On 2 January 1941, the *Luftwaffe* attacked the city and nearby Llandaff. During this nightmare raid 160 were killed. The cathedral at Llandaff received a direct hit. Gravestones were scattered far and wide and skulls and bones flew through the air.

PITIFUL PRISONS

The horrific history of the prisoners of war during the Second World War will make your hair stand on end or even turn it white overnight.

Good heavens, what's happened to you?

I read *Woeful Wales at War* before falling asleep last night!

Haden Spicer of Newport was imprisoned in Germany following the Normandy landings in 1944.

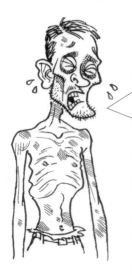

I hate talking about those days. I worked as a slave producing sugar for the Führer himself (Hitler was a sour old man!). Twelve hours a day, seven days a week (not good at sums? – that's 84 hours a week! Your lovely history teachers only work about 30 hours a week!). I had to shovel sugar beet into a grinding machine. And the food? We had to share one loaf of bread between five men! But on Christmas Day we had a white loaf instead of a black one! I lost a lot of weight. Thank goodness, the war was almost at an end. When I came back to Wales, a woman on the train asked me where I had been. I answered, and she replied, 'Well, you don't look too bad on it!' (I know where I'd like to send her!)

JOYLESS JAPANESE JAILERS

But the Japanese jails were the worst of all. They were
incredibly harsh. You could:

starve to death. David Ellis Roberts, a sailor
from Barmouth, ate weeds from the jungle
and stole banana skins from the pig trough because he
was so very, very hungry.

Let him have it.
It's not fit for pigs!

go mad because of the extreme cruelty.
Because there wasn't another Welshman in the
camp in Palembang on Sumatra island, Roberts
resorted to talking to himself (perhaps he got more
sense that way!).

die of dreadful diseases like beriberi (not enough
nutrition – well, there wasn't much in a banana
skin!) or dysentry (very, very, very loose diarrhoea).

be beaten with a bamboo cane by gruesome
guards – just for looking at them.

be beaten to death for not obeying the guards
(at least the teachers haven't tried this, yet!).
Brynley O. Thomas from Swansea witnessed the
punishment described on the next page:

Beware, all disobedient prisoners. If you refuse to obey the guards, your heads will be put into a wooden block and beaten to pulp with a bamboo cane. Then your body will be thrown into the sea for the sharks to devour.

THE MYSTERY OF HERR HESS ... SS

Britain's most famous prisoner of war was Rudolf (no, not Father Christmas's reindeer!) Hess, Hitler's deputy and a member of the SS (Adolf's own Secret Service of Soldiers ... sss!). Suddenly, on 10 May 1941, he fell out of the sky (well, he landed by parachute) in Scotland. He was caught by a farmservant wielding a pitchfork (the nervous Nazi seems to have forgotten his gun!) and imprisoned until 1945 in a military hospital in Abergavenny, south Wales.

No nonsense from you, Herr Hess ... ss!

Though he was a prisoner of war, he seems to have had a great time. The prison warder used to take him out for jolly jaunts to the town from time to time, or to visit the local castles, and even to enjoy a dinner with Lord Tredegar in Tredegar House!

Dear Adolf,
Having a happy holiday.
Pity you can't join me!

But at the end of the war he was sent back to Nuremberg in Germany to stand trial for war crimes. He was found guilty and imprisoned for life.

But WHY had Hess flown to Scotland in the first place? That is the mega mystery.

✠ Had Hitler sent him to discuss peace terms with Britain?
✠ Did some British politicians (and even King George himself?) want to get rid of Churchill as prime minister?
✠ Had Hess come of his own free will in order to please Hitler? Apparently he adored his boss the Führer!
✠ Was Hess mad? He claimed he couldn't remember any of his own horrible history!

BUT the most difficult question of all:

✠ Was this man actually Herr Rudolf Hess or was he
   an impostor?

But my pants prove I'm Herr Hess!

R. HESS

And it's still a mega mystery! And we won't be able to
solve this problem until we see the government's
confidential papers (at present they're kept safe in a safe
somewhere), or until we dig up Herr Hess's grave and
test his DNA. (Now, where's that spade?)

THE PATHETIC BALLAD OF THE ARANDORA STAR

Some of the prisoners of war in Britain had evil
experiences too. Here is one story about Italian
prisoners or war. Sing this ballad with gusto – but not
in front of Italians!

> Now listen, take heed of my story
> Of a luxury liner, so brave,
> She was hit by a German torpedo,
> And she sank to a watery grave!
> On board there were hundreds of prisoners
> From Italy, Germany too,
> And, forming a military escort,
> Guards from Wales were part of the crew.

Italians had flocked to the Valleys
In the days when Victoria was Queen,
Their cafés and parlours were famous
For coffee and cakes and ice cream.
They quickly made friends with the locals:
Rabiotti and Chezzi and Rees,
Sharing *cawl* and *spaghetti* and *losin*,
Which was great – whilst the world was at peace.

But when fighting erupted in Europe
Those friends became foes in a trice,
And Churchill proclaimed, full of venom,
That Italians were not very nice.
'They're Fascists, they're cruel and dangerous,★
They do not deserve to live free,
We must punish their leader, Benito,
That infamous Mussol-i-ni.'

The weak and the feeble were captured
And taken, with barely a cry,
Before they could pack up their teddies
Or kiss all their loved ones goodbye.
The captives were pushed below hatches,
But no Red Cross Flag was flown
To warn that the *Star* carried prisoners
And that U-boats should leave her alone.

A German boat sighted its target,
Then fired on the enemy ship,
The vessel was hit on the starboard
And immediately started to dip.
No time to find safety in lifeboats,
They jumped for their lives, if they dared,
The water was choked with bodies and oil:
Not many survivors were spared.

Eight hundred were drowned altogether,
And those who escaped with their lives
Were sent to Australian prisons,
With never a word to their wives . . .
'Ciao!' they called. *'Arrivederci!'***
As the cruise ship departed the quay.
But wrecked lies the *Arandora Star*
At the bottom of the Irish Sea.

But in 2010 a memorial was unveiled in Cardiff to
remember the 53 Welsh Italians who were on board the
Arandora Star – BENE! BRAVO!

★ Many young Italians were fighting in the British army – and they
weren't spiteful spies at all! Most of the Italians on board the ship were
innocent old men.

★★ *Ciao*! – you have to pronounce it 'Chow!' – means 'goodbye'. So
does *Arrivederci*! 'Arry-ve-dair-chee'.

LA CASA DI DIO (or 'God's House' to you and me)

But some of the Italians had a warmer welcome in Wales, although they were prisoners of war.

These were soldiers captured in Africa and brought to Henllan, near Llandysul. There were 1,500 of them. During the day they worked on the surrounding farms and at night they yearned for Italy and its way of life (the weather, pizzas, opera singing, wine – can you blame them?). These prisoners were Catholics and they decided to turn one of their miserable wooden prison huts into a church.

To transform a wooden hut into a church you must collect all kinds of rubbish:

- empty food boxes to build an altar
- corned-beef tins to make candlesticks
- cement bags for altar cloths
- vegetable peelings and tea leaves to dye water to paint the walls
- one amazing artist.

LLAN-NON
LLAN-PONG

And they found just such an artist – Mario Ferlito, who painted a fantastic mural of Jesus Christ's Last Supper (the prisoners would probably have enjoyed some fresh bread and wine too!), and it's still there!

KISSES AND CUDDLES

Reach for your tissues – this section is very weepy-weepy. Some Italian and German prisoners of war fell head over heels in love with Welsh girls (hardly surprising because they're so pretty!) and they decided to marry them and stay in Wales! But remember, the girls' families weren't always happy with this (would you be? – with the prisoners having to wear horrible brown overalls covered in yellow circles!), especially if the men were German. Several Welsh girls and their secret sweethearts were bullied and harassed by local people. Edna Stenger from Fishguard describes how she and her German boyfriend Karl, were bullied by the locals:

Crowds of local lads used to come to the dance on Saturday night and they used to bump into us on purpose – bump, bump, all the time. Karl had become good friends with the town policeman. He was standing at the door one evening and he saw what was going on. And he gave those lads a right telling-off. We were left in peace after that.

Prisoners led eventful lives! Some (both British and German) were brilliant at escaping from their prisons.

Three Tries for the Welshman from Barmouth!
The Sensational Story of our Headstrong Hero!

CORPORAL CYRIL MORRIS'S story is quite sensational. He managed to escape, not ONCE, not TWICE, but THREE TIMES from the grip of the Germans and the Italians.

In 1942 Morris and 34,999 soldiers were captured by the enemy in Tobruk, Libya in north Africa (this proves that this was a World War!), and taken to a prison in Italy. In this prison our bold hero joined the choir called 'The Men of Harlech'!

Please let me join. I do come from Barmouth!

Once!

But then came a chance to escape. Mussolini, the Italian leader, had just been sacked and everything in the prison was topsy-turvey. Morris sneaked out and was sheltered by an Italian family (who weren't too keen on Mussolini's antics either!).

Then, according to Morris's own description, 'I was captured again, and put on a cattle train bound for Germany.' (Boo-Moo!)

Twice!

And then he saw an opportunity to escape for a second time – he jumped off the train and hid in the mountains. Unfortunately a spiteful spy was hiding there too and betrayed him. He was caught – again.

The joyless Jerries (or Germans) took his shoes off this time (what a stink and no hope of escaping now!) and put him back on a train bound for Germany.

Thrice!

'But then,' Morris explained, 'the train was bombed by US planes. I, and several other prisoners, jumped out and we found some Italians who were willing to help us.'

But how did Morris get home?

'I met some British soldiers on the road one day. They just couldn't believe my story until I said I came from Barmouth. One of them knew the town. Thank goodness – Barmouth for ever!'

Yes, indeed. Barmouthians (a clever name for Barmouth people) manage to reach every corner of the world! Congratulations to our headstrong hero!

Hip, Hip, Hooray to Morris, the exceptional escapologist!

The Spectacular Scandal of the Prisoners at Island Farm

For shame, for shame, Bridgend. You have let 70 important Nazis, the most dangerous and villainous German nasties, ESCAPE from Island Farm prison. How on earth did they manage to do so? What were the guards doing? Sleeping? Why hadn't the guard dogs stopped them? We want answers to these questions or we won't be able to sleep soundly at night.

A TREACHEROUS TUNNEL

The guards have discovered an 18-metre long tunnel leading from one of the prison huts under the barbed-wire fence around the camp. Tommy Hughes, one of the guards, said that prisoners had been stealing knives and forks to dig the tunnel, and milk and meat tins to make a pipe to bring air into it.

the legs off their beds to make props to hold up the tunnel roof. And we believe the diggers worked naked or we might have noticed mud stains on their clothes.'

We have to ask – did these guards notice anything? What is the standard of our guards? This is a spectacularly serious scandal!

DISGRACEFUL GUARD DOGS

And what on earth happened to the guard dogs? They say they were tricked with curry powder!

Why are they eating cawl with their hands?

Mmm-m I smell curry!

I fancy some rabbit curry for supper!

'We didn't hear any noise,' said red-faced Tommy, 'because the prisoners sang loudly to disguise the sound of digging. And we hadn't noticed the soil from the tunnel because they hid it behind a false wall and down the toilet (it's lucky the toilets hadn't blocked or it would have made a right mess!). They sawed

But we can be glad of one thing. The woeful warders managed to stop some prisoners from escaping. And it won't be long before they catch the rest of them, will it?

123

19 March 1945   **The Bridgend Free Press**

Island Farm celebrates!

Every prisoner under lock and key once more!

Yes, the guards at Island Farm can celebrate with a grand party tonight. Every nasty German villain is back behind prison bars.

> We won't need to dig a tunnel this time!

> I guessed they weren't from round here because I hadn't seen them before. And all they said to one another was *'Bitte, Bitte'*. Well, it's not all that bitter at this time of the year, is it? Very strange, I thought to myself.

Two of the cheeky chaps had hidden on a goods train and had got as far as Southampton! And another four had stolen a doctor's car to travel to Cardiff and had caught a train to Birmingham! And – it seems that some of the gullible guards had actually helped these prisoners to escape by pushing the car when it refused to start! The prisoners had drawn maps on their handkerchiefs and prepared very clever false documents.

Over in Cwm-gwrach three of the escaped prisoners caught a local bus. But as Dai Full Pelt said:

It's lucky that the Welshmen on the bus were brighter than the prison guards. These cheeky chaps won't be on another bus for a very long time!

Let's hope this inexcusable error will be a warning to all. The war is NOT over yet!

FUN AND GAMES ON THE HOME FRONT

During the Second World War, being at home was almost as exciting as being overseas fighting the enemy, because the war reached every nook and cranny of the country. One poor schoolgirl's home in London was destroyed by a bomb so she was sent as an evacuee to live safely in Bwlch-gwyn, near Wrexham. And then, two bombs fell in the field in front of the house where she was staying! (Boom, boom! What bad luck!)

WAS THERE A WARM WELCOME IN THE HILLSIDE?

Everyone in the WORLD knows that Welsh people love making cups of tea and Welsh cakes for visitors. And in 1940 the wonderful, welcoming song 'We'll Keep a Welcome in the Hillside' was composed. It's not surprising that all the women and children from the cities of England looked forward to a grand tea party when they arrived in Wales as evacuees at the beginning of the sad Second World War.

BUT ... did everyone have a warm welcome in the hillside? Mmmm ... perhaps you'd better read these letters – before you decide.

Somewhere at the end of
the world
15 November 1939

Dear Gran'ma,

   I hope you're all right and that
Grampa is busy putting all the bombs
and fires out in Liverpool. I'm staying
with a very miserable old woman. She
speaks Welsh to me all the time. I
don't understand a word she says and
she doesn't understand a word I say
either. I'm terribly homesick, Gran'ma.
I've started to wee the bed again and I
don't know what to do.
   I'm tired now, because Mrs Jones
makes me wash the floor before going
to school every morning.

Good or bad night!
Your tearful little granddaughter,
Winnie

(not Winnie the Pooh but
Winnie Wee-wee) xxx

Bangor,
20 November 1939

Dear Mr Jones,

I hope you're busy killing the wicked Jerries*. I'm not feeling too well. Because I have some empty rooms in the house I've been forced to take an evacuee from Liverpool to stay with me. Well, Mr Jones, you'll never believe what a nuisance she is. When she arrived all she had in her brown paper bag was one set of spare clothes, a comb and a toothbrush. Her clothes were in tatters and, worse still, they were full of lice and nits! I've had to wash them all and then force her to stand naked under the cold-water tap in the yard. And now she's started to wet the bed! I need the patience of a saint. Thank goodness we have no children, Mr Jones.

Your dear and hardworking wife,
Mrs Jones

* Jerries was a nickname used for Germans.

5 December 1939

Dear Gran'ma,

It's me again. Do you remember me saying that my homesickness for Liverpool is making me wet the bed? Well, I've had such a row about this from Mrs Jones! But I've found a way to hide it now. I use Teddy to dry the wee and then I wring him dry out of the bedroom window.

I hate the food here – she gives me some horrible soup called *cawl* every day. It's like pigswill! I'd love to have a packet of chips instead. One day she gave me nettle tea! It was absolutely horrible!

I had an awful row yesterday. I know you don't want me to make any effort to learn Welsh, but I asked the girls next door to teach me how to say 'Good morning' and 'Good night' nicely. They taught me to tell Mrs Jones to '*Cer i grafu*' in the morning and '*Cer i gosi*' at night*. But she went crackers! I've no idea why – I was only being polite! She's coming now – I'd better go.
Lots of kisses,
Your silly little granddaughter,
Winnie Wee-wee

* Poor little Winnie. '*Cer i grafu*' means 'Go and scratch' and '*Cer i gosi*' means 'Go and itch'!

BANG!

BANG!

Perhaps wee Winnie might have been better off here in Liverpool with all the bombs than safe in faraway Wales!

Bangor   20 December 1939

Dear Mr Jones,

I was glad to hear that you'd enjoyed the Welsh cakes I sent you in the food parcel. It would be nice to say that the evacuee is eating well too, but she turns up her nose at my cabbage soup and she refuses to even taste the red beetroot cake. What's wrong with the little minx? I've taught her how to eat neatly with a knife and fork at last instead of with her hands. I've started taking her to chapel with me three times on a Sunday. She'll have to sit still for hours there!

Our Father . . . Give us this day our daily bread . . . please?

And at last her skin is looking better too -
I've scrubbed and scrubbed it under the
cold-water tap! She's starting to learn some
proper Welsh now too. She said Bradà (Bore da)
and 'Tö star (Nos da) yesterday! I'm sure she
won't dare to swear at me ever again.

Thank goodness, I get seven shillings and
sixpence a week for keeping her. I'm trying to
save some of this money to buy a little present
for you. Winnie will never know.

Your cunning wifey,
Mrs Jones

And there you are – two sides to the argument.
Was EVERY evacuee happy in Wales during the sad
Second World War? Did EVERYONE welcome them
warmly? What do you think?

Of course, some parts of Wales, like Swansea, Cardiff
and Pembroke Dock, weren't safe for evacuees nor for
the people who lived there either because of all the
bombing. Lots of people from Swansea slept rough on
Fairwood Common during the terrible bombing in
February 1941, and there was no one left in Pembroke
Dock some nights.

That was easy — everyone's run away. The town's empty!

TRUE OR FALSE
HELP! THE ENEMY HAS LANDED

Everyone was frightened stiff that the enemy would land in Britain during the war. And so the Home Guard (or Dad's Army) was established. Many spiteful stories are told about this 'army':

> *Ha ha ha! Hee hee hee!*
> *Let's have a laugh at Dad's Army!*

But were these stories **true** or **false?**
✔ Tick the correct boxes.

	True	False
1. Everyone was afraid of a BLITZKRIEG – Germany defeating Britain and landing on the beaches of Wales, and paratroops parachuting in without warning. By 1939, the Germans had invaded Poland, Norway, the Netherlands, Belgium and France. And every fit man in Britain was in the armed forces already. That's why, in 1940, the Home Guard was established.		

	True	False
2. You didn't have to be fighting fit to be in Dad's Army.		
3. Every member of the adventurous army was given a super uniform.		
4. They also had wonderful new weapons.		
5. While they were practising with these wonderful weapons members of the 'Army' shot ordinary people stone dead.		
6. In order to totally confuse any enemy army which landed in the Welsh countryside, Dad's Army removed roadsigns and burned maps.		
7. Every member of Dad's Army had to practise hiding in bushes and woods.		
8. The Germans had their own version of Dad's Army – the VOLKSSTURM (or, the 'people's storm' – what a thunderingly good name!).		

I can't remember which way to go home now!

1.**TRUE** Church bells were supposed to ring out if the Germans were invading. On 7 September 1940 there were rumours that the enemy had landed on Llandudno beach. One man ran out in his pyjamas to try to stop them! But the story was false. Then, on 28 September, in Gowerton near Swansea, someone heard men whispering from the bog near the river. But were they speaking Welsh, English or German? That was the question. The hardworking Home Guard searched the bog (not the toilet!) through the night but without any luck. Then, in the morning, what did they find? A group of local men out shooting wild ducks. They had been caught by the incoming tide!

Halt! Friend or Foe?

Duck! Don't shoot! Quack, quack!

The people of Merthyr Tydfil were afraid that the enemy would land on the Brecon Beacons and pull the plug out of the huge reservoir there and drown the whole of Merthyr!

This was the government's advice on what to do if the enemy landed:
If you happen to be standing behind a tree with a grenade or a bomb in your hand and a car comes past full of enemy officers, even if your best friend is driving the car YOU MUST THROW THE BOMB AT THE CAR. That's what your friend would want you to do! (Oh yeah?)

2.**TRUE** You didn't have to see any doctor, and any man (no women, of course) between 17 and 65 years old who could move freely' could join the Home Guard. Many members of this army had fought and had been injured in the First World War.

I'll be useful in the Home Guard because I can see who's coming behind me!

8.**TRUE** And the Germans were even more hopeless! They had no uniforms or weapons. (But, of course, Britain was not about to invade Germany!)

Ych a fi – this colour just doesn't suit me!

coming.
had to crawl through cowpats! The enemy could have smelled them
learned to crawl on their stomachs around the countryside. Often they
from the enemy. They practised guerilla (not gorilla) tactics and they
7.**A HALF TRUTH** They used leaves and twigs to disguise themselves
the seashore.
also learned how to fire the huge guns in the underground forts built on
6.**TRUE** And they put coils of barbed wire along the beaches too. They

hair turned white overnight – poor dab – and her leg went bad too!
years old) was shot in the leg. His leg rotted and he died. His wife's
his rifle! And Robert Leslie Howell (32
quite know how to load bullets into
dead by a sloppy soldier who didn't
Madeleine Silly from Sully) was shot
Madeleine Selley from Barry (no, not
by careless members of the Home Guard.
course, and several people were shot
5.**TRUE** The weapons weren't brilliant, of

Who needs enemies when you've got friends like these?

were petrified of this hazardous bomb!
a coalmine in south Wales. Everyone, even the Home Guard themselves,
a hand bomb called the Kerridge Cucumber made by a blacksmith in
make their own weapons – wooden truncheons with iron spikes and
Farmers lent them shotguns and rifles. Some clever members tried to
4.**FALSE** They only had knives, pitchforks, brushes and farm implements.

Later on, each member was given a smart new uniform.
3.**FALSE** In the beginning the only uniforms they had were armbands.

REMARKABLE SECOND WORLD WAR RULES

1. Everyone must have a gas mask

This will save you from gases and smoke
Which might otherwise cause you to choke,
So don't be a dunce,
Wear your gas mask at once,
Although breathing is hardly a joke!

The Air-raid Wardens (very, very important busybodies) were supposed to let everyone know if there was going to be a gas attack by rattling gas rattles loudly (like football hooligans!). And, when the danger was over, they had to ring a bell. (But what if you lived far away, on Snowdon? You would probably die of gas poisoning! Gas-p, gas-p!)

Everyone hated wearing gas masks. But schoolchildren soon realised they could make dodgy noises and rude smells by blowing through their Mickey Mouse masks.

By the end of 1939, 38 million gas masks had been distributed. And what was the war's best joke? No one needed to use a gas mask during the sad Second World War! ('Eek!' squeaked Mickey Mouse!)

2. Don't show any light to the enemy:

After dark when the stars filled the sky,
Round the houses the wardens would pry,
Searching all night
For slivers of light
Which the enemy bombers could spy.

The Air-raid wardens loved punishing those who didn't cover their windows with boring black blackout curtains and tape them down tightly on all sides. They had to ensure that no light or anything white shone out to attract the enemy bombers.

Some said that the German bombers had been drawn to attack Swansea in 1941 by a sly spy shining a mirror on Kilvey hill. The town's wild women heard this story and off they went to the spy's home, armed with sticks ready to (almost) kill him. Can you blame them?

3. You must carry an identity card:

Your identity card you must carry
So that questions you'll easily parry.
When you hear 'Friend or foe?'
You will instantly know
That it's YOU, and not Tom, Dick or Harry!

4. When the bombing begins, run to hide in a shelter:

When the air-raid siren starts braying,
You must hide where you can – no more playing! –
Under tables or chairs,
Even under the stairs,
And then, if you're wise, you'll start praying!

The Anderson shelters★ are grotty,
And at night they can drive you quite dotty,
But with blankets galore,
Tea and biscuits and more,
You'll survive – but remember your potty!

★ Two million Anderson shelters were built in gardens during the sad Second World War. Six people (and the odd cat and dog and parrot and goldfish!) could squash into one shelter.

You could be stuck in the shelter for hours!

But, of course, if you were ill in hospital (perhaps you'd lost a leg in an air raid) the most ridiculous rule was: Hide under your pillow, put an enamel bowl over your head and pray. (Very lame advice!)

5. You must listen to the 9 o'clock news on the radio every night:

(Well, it wasn't a RULE exactly, but everyone did this.)

> *To find out if we're likely to lose*
> *Tune in to the nine o'clock news,*
> *   But you'll have to speak English*
> *   Or a smattering of Wenglish,*
> *To appreciate Churchill's strong views!*

There were only three and a half hours of Welsh-language programmes a week on the radio in 1940! The Mountain Ash National Eisteddfod was held on the radio in 1940, because of the war, and in 1943, items from an eisteddfod in Cairo (Egypt!) were broadcast on the radio. When John Evans, Brynsiencyn, sang 'Cartref' (Home) at this eisteddfod, everyone was in floods of tears (hardly a surprise!).

There's nowhere like 'Home Sweet Home!'

No indeed, there isn't.

But there were items in English about Wales on the radio –
especially 'Dai's Letters to the Troops' – entertaining
letters intended to lift the hearts of homesick soldiers
all over the world. And in 1940 the BBC moved its
light entertainment programmes (full of fun and jolly
hockey sticks) to Penrhyn Hall, Bangor, because of the
bombing. When they were recording one of these light
programmes a heavy bomb fell on the hall (Bang!
Crash!), but the show went on, of course!

The drums are very loud tonight!

ROTTEN, ROTTEN RATIONING

If all the bombing, the blackout, the evacuees and the
constant fear got everyone down, then you could cheer
them all up by inviting them to a brilliant banquet.
However . . .

Problem 1

You would have to remember that lots of foodstuffs,
such as meat, butter, cheese, margarine, sugar, tea, sweets,
yes sweets (at least this would be good for your teeth),
and eggs, were rationed, and that only very, very small
amounts of these foods were allowed per person a week.

This was because the German U-boats bombed all the ships which carried food to Britain (how mean was that?!). There wasn't any popcorn either, so the children of Garndolbenmaen took gooseberries to eat in the cinema. One lady from Swansea described how she coped, poor thing:

I spent hours every day just STARING at an empty box of Black Magic chocolates we had at home – trying to imagine the taste of an 'Orange Cup' or a 'Coffee Cream'!

Problem 2

There were almost NO bananas or oranges available throughout the woeful war. When oranges arrived in a shop, women and children would have to queue for hours to buy some. Lots of people ate the orange peel as well as the actual fruit (*Ych a fi*!). When the headteacher of Nevern school showed the children a banana, they were frightened. Did they go bananas, I wonder?!

Come back – it's only a banana!

No Problem 1

You could keep hens and pigs in your garden and you would have plenty of eggs and bacon (and droppings and pig muck!).

No Problem 2

You could become bosom pals with a fruitful farmer and perhaps he would let you have a side of ham or a dozen eggs – but don't tell anyone. Be prepared to pay (lots and lots of money!) for them on the black market. (Farmers aren't stupid!) A woman from Pontardawe described how they would carry dead pigs around in coffins in case meddlesome officials found out about this secret swapping.

I think you've got a pig in that coffin.

No, no. that's Gran'ma!

No Problem 3

You could dig for victory! Dig the garden and grow your own vegetables and fruit. Follow the example of Doctor Carrot and Potato Pete – great favourites during the Second World War.

'Grow carrots, for without any question,'
Said the Doctor, 'they're good for digestion,
 And on top of all that,
  You'll see like a cat
In the dark.' What a splendid suggestion!

A MAGNIFICENT MENU FOR A BRILL SECOND WORLD WAR BANQUET

Savoury stuff

A choice of sandwich fillings:

Condensed milk (very slushy)

Spam (poor man's ham)

Bananas

(OK, so there weren't any bananas – you'll just have to make the banana filling by mashing boiled parsnips and banana essence together. Ych a fi!)

Stuffed ears (What?)

Fried fish

(make your own fish by mixing milk, ground rice, butter and potatoes together, shape this mixture like a fish, coat with breadcrumbs and fry – it will be good enough to swim in the river Taff!)

Beetroot pudding

Enough for 4 people: 6 ounces (war measurements) of whole meal flour, ½ a teaspoon of baking powder, 1 ounce of sugar, 4 ounces of grated beetroot, ½ an ounce of margarine. Rub the margarine into the flour and the baking powder. Add the sugar and beetroot. Then add 2–3 spoonfuls of milk. Cook for 35 minutes. This is very tasty (?) hot or cold (or in the bin!).

Coffee

No coffee? Grind some barley seeds and acorns, and then add boiled water (don't worry if it tastes like rubber).

If you're off-colour, ill or at death's door after eating this brill banquet – bless you!

TALENTED TRACTORS

All farmers fell in love with the talented tractor during the Second World War because they were expected to grow more, and more and more food crops.

DIG FOR VICTORY!

'Increase the yield of every field'

Buy a TRACTOR, now

It does the work of 5 horses
No need to clean up dung or pee
Cost: £175 (the price of 59 lambs!)
Plenty of diesel (only petrol is rationed!)

You can plough through the day and night.

REMARKABLE RECYCLING

This was every child's helpful hobby during the war –
collecting every spare piece of metal – gates, rails, and
saucepans to make Spitfires (fighter planes) and
Wellingtons to bomb the Germans and anyone else in
the way.

Sosban fach – let's turn it into scrap,
Sosban fawr – let's bomb them off the map.
And *cawl's* off the menu, Johnny *bach*!

You'll know this song if you're a Scarlets' fan or you
come from Llanelli.

SIX SILLY TIPS

Would you like to be the flashy star of the fashion world during the war? Of course you would! Follow these six silly tips and you will be the star ★ of the show.

1. Are you worried that the seat of your knickers or your pants is wearing thin. (You must be careful or everyone will be able to see right through them!) Yes? Then follow *Mrs Sew and Sew*'s impressive instructions. Mend them with a pretty patch. They should be fine.

Today Johnny and Janet are wearing the latest fashion . . .

2. Not enough material to made a beautiful wedding gown? You have two charming choices:

- get married in your war uniform (made from material which scratches and itches and in an ugly khaki-brown or dingy-blue colour) OR
- steal a parachute (but don't get carried away!) – the super satin will make a great wedding dress.

You'll never guess what material I used for my wedding gown!

3. No silk stockings to wear to a dance or a trip to the cinema with your favourite soldier? You have two more charming choices:

• find an American soldier who's very homesick for America (you'd never guess!) and give him a smacking big kiss. He'll have his pockets full of lovely silk stockings and he'll give them all to you (because his true love is so far away over the ocean waves . . . ! Boo hoo!).

• paint your legs brown with gravy browning or tea, and ask your best friend to mark a slick seam down the back of your leg with a dark brown pencil. BUT there may be a problem – don't go out when it's raining or when there are hungry hounds around!

Gr-rr, gr-rr-avy! Mmmm – very tasty. Yes, I am a [wo]man's best friend!

4. No hair gel to keep your hair stiff (very fashionable in 1943)? Mix some water and sugar together and pour the mixture over your hair. Within an hour you will be able to skate on it! But don't go out in the rain – your hair will be a complete flop!

5. No lipstick to brighten your lips? Use beetroot juice! (But don't be sick!)

6. No money to buy shiny new shoes? Put a piece of cardboard inside each shoe to hide the holes and cut away the front – peep-po, big toe (but don't cut your toes off by mistake!).

BEVIN'S BRAINY PLAN

During the sad Second World War (just like during the wasteful First World War) there was a huge demand for Welsh coal as fuel for the naval ships, the trains, the factories, and to keep everyone as snug as a bug in a rug during the winter months. But by 1943 thousands of miners had ESCAPED from the coalmines to fight in the army. Somehow other workers had to be found to replace them. That's when brainy Ernest Bevin (the Minister of Labour) came up with a practical plan to solve the problem:

BEVIN'S NOTEWORTHY NOTEBOOK

A. Force young boys to become coalminers.

B. Draw a raffle to choose which boys will join the army and which will have to go down the mines.

Congratulations on winning the raffle.

But I didn't want to be a miner!

C. Give them hobnailed boots and helmets but no pick and shovel. (How very stupid – they will have to use their hands to dig coal!)

D. If they refuse to work in the coalmines they will have to pay a huge fine (lots of money), or be sent to prison. (Boo-hoo!)

E. WARNING – New miners MUST NOT BE TOLD that:
  • the work will be very hard, the hours long and all for little pay! Alan Jennings was a Bevin Boy in the Albion coalmine:

The shaft went down 640 metres and at the bottom I had to walk 2 miles to reach the coalface. The roof was only 106 centimetes high and we could never stand up straight. We worked 6 days a week, getting up at 5 in the morning and finishing the shift at 2.30 in the afternoon. We all washed together and that was the first time I had seen hundreds of naked men all in the same place!!

Well, well, I hadn't realised that coalminers had white faces!

• the real miners will have a good laugh at the new ones. One rather mean miner said:

It's a pity that the Bevin Boys weren't poured down the drain with the dirty water!

• that a quarter of all miners are killed (squashed to death by drams or falling coal, suffocated by gas . . . you choose!) or they injure their fingers, their hands or their eyes.

Would you like to die in a coalmine or in the army? YOU choose.

• after the war no one will thank them for working so hard.

Wasn't it brilliant being a Bevin Boy!

WOMEN DURING THE SAD SECOND WORLD WAR - OUT OF THAT KITCHEN, NOW!

Yes, this was another chance for women to shine. But some were very confused:

1900–14	1914–18	1918–39	1939–45
In the kitchen	Out of the kitchen	In the kitchen	Out of the kitchen

In out, in out – I don't know where I should be!

And there was NO choice – every woman HAD to register for work (or else!).

WHERE?

👄 In the Land Army (as in the First World War – read all about it under 'The Wonderful Women of the First World War') milking cows, cleaning out filthy cowsheds, sawing huge trees and catching rats.

- Back in the Munitions Factories making dangerous explosives and bombs. In Bridgend 35,000, most of them women, worked at the enormous munitions factory. During her first week in work there, an explosive exploded in Gwen Obern's hand and she was blinded for life (poor thing).
- Making aeroplanes – Wellington bombers in Broughton, Flintshire, and sea planes in Beaumaris.

Many of the women enjoyed working outside the home – they had more money and lots of company and fun. In the Munitions Factory in Bangor they had a choir. And their favourite song? 'There'll always be an England!' (In Wales!)

Fashion in the Factory

In spite of the dirt, oil and dust, the women still tried to look fashionable (or that's what they believed anyway!).

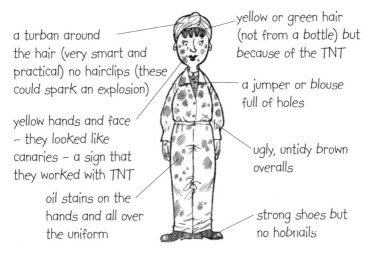

yellow or green hair (not from a bottle) but because of the TNT

a turban around the hair (very smart and practical) no hairclips (these could spark an explosion)

a jumper or blouse full of holes

yellow hands and face – they looked like canaries – a sign that they worked with TNT

ugly, untidy brown overalls

oil stains on the hands and all over the uniform

strong shoes but no hobnails

OR

👄 In the Armed Forces, and this was the order of importance:

the WRNS – Navy girls. THEY were the *crachach* (the posh ones) at the TOP of the ladder.

the WAAFS – Air-force girls, full of glamour (and the pilots weren't bad-looking either)

the ATS – ordinary women in the Army. Most Welsh girls joined the ATS.

But, of course, these women didn't actually fight at all! (Oh, NO!). They had to drive important men around, work in the offices or look after the distribution of goods. Some people complained that these women were too 'friendly' with the soldiers, the sailors and the pilots (*Ych a fi*!) – and especially with the Americans who stayed in camps around Wales. And we don't mean just asking them for chewing gum: 'Got any gum, chum?' Oh no! Some of the girls married GI (not Gorgeous and Innocent but Government Issue!) soldiers, and went to live in America when the war was over. (And that's the end of that little story!)

And also:

- Many became nurses in hospitals in Britain and abroad. They saw and heard some awful things.
- The girls who were in the air-raid service had to clear bombs, extinguish fires and look after those who had been injured.
- And after coming home from work, all the washing, cleaning, ironing and cooking was still there waiting to be done (who else could have done it after all?).

Once again there were a few conscientious objectors – CONCHIES – who refused altogether to have anything to do with the war effort. Maedwen Daniel from Godre'r Graig, in the Swansea valley, was a super singer but she refused to sing in any concert to raise money for the war. She was brought before a tribunal of very important men and punished by being made to clean the chapel! (This probably helped to polish her singing too!)

GOOD OR BAD? THE COMPLEX CONSEQUENCES OF THE SAD SECOND WORLD WAR

Yes, the 1939–45 War affected every part of the world and even the best history teachers won't be able to list all its effects. But here are some of the bad and some of the good effects. You choose.

1. The world was divided into west (America and her friends) and east (Russia and her friends) and this was the beginning of the COLD war. Very bad for everyone concerned.

2. The Soviet Union (Russia) conquered all the countries of eastern Europe: Czechoslovakia, Hungary, Latvia, Poland, Estonia, Lithuania ... and forced them to become Communists (ask your teachers to explain this!) for 40 years. BAD for these poor countries, but GOOD for Russia!

3. To pay her back for starting the war Germany was divided into east and west, and in Berlin they built a huge Wall to divide the city into two. It wasn't taken down until 1989. BAD for the Germans and Berliners but GOOD for the other powers?

The number of those who tried to escape from the east to the west = 5,000
The number of those who died while trying = about 200
The number of those who tried to escape from the west to the east = 0.

Eastern soldiers sit on the wall,
Eastern soldiers shoot one and all,
All of the women and all of the men:
Berliners escaping to freedom again.

4. The Jews were given their own country in Israel (where their roots were), although the Palestinians had lived there for many centuries. BAD for the Palestinians and GOOD for the Jews. And they're still fighting over this land today.

5. The United Nations was established to try to prevent more woeful wars like this one. GOOD, but what about the wars in Korea, Vietnam, Iraq and Afghanistan, Rwanda and . . . ?

6. New technologies were developed, which would transform the world: nuclear power, computers (Hooray!) and the jet engine (Hooray again!). EXCELLENT.

7. And in Britain, the National Health Service was established to give everyone access to a free health service from the cradle to the grave. EXCELLENT INDEED – and whose idea was it, we wonder? The Welshman, Aneurin Bevan, of course.

'DAS ENDE!'
(The End – Thank Goodness!)

It's time, at last, to bring to a close
The history of wars and their wearisome woes.

To end our tale of merciless strife,
The terrible trenches, the loss of life,

The bombing of innocents, score upon score,
The suffering, the grieving, the prisoners of war,

The thousands of soldiers from Wales who died
In senseless slaughter, through national pride.

But – lest we forget – we need to discuss
Who won the wars. Was it THEM or US?

And agree, as we share the horror and pain,
That 'victory with honour' no one can claim.

For war never tells us who's wrong or who's right,
Just who's left standing at the end of the fight.

And now let us strive for a better way,
And hail peace, not war, each Remembrance Day.

Also available:

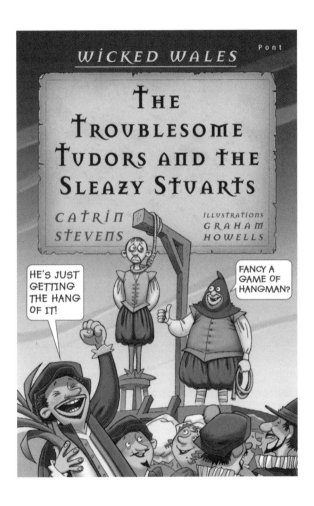